MARTIN LUTHER KING

MARTIN LUTHER KING

The Inconvenient Hero

_____

Vincent Harding

ORBIS BOOKS

Maryknoll, New York 10545

Ninth printing, January 2007

The Catholic Foreign Mission Society of America (Maryknoll) recruits and trains people for overseas missionary service. Through Orbis Books, Maryknoll aims to foster the international dialogue that is essential to mission. The books published, however, reflect the opinions of their authors and are not meant to represent the official position of the society.

The publishers gratefully acknowledge the publications in which many of these essays, in different form, originally appeared: chapter 1, "The Inconvenient Hero," was originally published in *Union Seminary Quarterly* 4 (1986); chapter 2, "Getting Ready for the Hero," was originally published in *Sojourners,* January 1986; chapter 3, "Martin King, Burning Bushes, and Us," was originally published in the *National Leader,* September 1, 1983; chapter 4, "Beyond Amnesia," was originally published in *The Journal of American History* 74, no. 2 (September, 1987); chapter 5, "The Land Beyond," was originally published in *Sojourners,* January 1983; chapter 6, "We Must Keep Going," was originally published in *Fellowship,* January/February 1987; chapter 8, "Tell the Children," was originally published in *Parenting,* December/January 1991.

Queries regarding rights and permissions should be addressed to: Orbis Books, P. O. Box 308, Maryknoll, New York 10545-0308.

Manufactured in the United States of America

ORBIS / ISBN 1-57075-064-5

CONTENTS

Introduction   **vii**

1   The Inconvenient Hero:
The Last Years of Martin Luther King, Jr.   **1**

2   Getting Ready for the Hero   **23**

3   Martin King, Burning Bushes, and Us:
Revisiting the March on Washington   **45**

4   Beyond Amnesia:
Martin Luther King, Jr., and the Future of America   **58**

5   The Land Beyond:
Reflections on King's "Beyond Vietnam" Speech   **69**

6   We Must Keep Going   **82**

7   Blessed Astronaut of the Human Race   **116**

8   Tell the Children   **128**

Epilogue   **139**

Notes   **143**

SETTING THE CAPTIVE(S) FREE

This work is an experiment in healing, an attempt to explore and address the profound sense of national amnesia that has distorted so much of America's approach to Martin Luther King, our national hero. Most of these essays on King and the nation were developed during the years of our intense discussion and debate concerning the meaning of this man's life and work for a country that is still unclear about who he was, what we expect of him as hero, and what he might expect and demand of us.

As I reflected on the image of King that was consistently emerging from the national conversations and celebrations, it seemed clear to me that one of our crucial difficulties in apprehending the meaning of the man and the movement he represented was rooted in our apparent determination to forget—or ignore—the last years of his life. Somehow it appeared as if we were determined to hold this hero captive to the powerful period of his life that culminated in the magnificent March on Washington of 1963, refusing to allow him to break out beyond the stunning eloquence of "I Have a Dream." For reasons that I attempt to explore in this collection, we Americans have insisted that King live forever in the unbroken sunlight of that historic August day on the Mall when hundreds of thousands of us stood in that place, and millions more gathered before television sets across the nation, to affirm our solidarity with his vision of racial harmony and triumphant freedom.

Somehow, King seemed easier to manage as a hero, to explain to our children, our congresspeople, and ourselves if we could forget the search for economic justice that had already begun to emerge in the March's official purpose, "for Jobs and Freedom," and if we could ignore the shadows that were soon to be cast across King's life (and many others) by the white terrorist bombing that killed four Sunday school children in Birmingham, just weeks after the March. As the official national celebrations began, evoking powerful memories of the courage, religious faith, and astounding levels of personal and societal renewal that were promised and manifested in the Southern-based freedom movement, I knew at the same time that we had chosen to forget other vital manifestations of the American democratic hope that King represented.

His creative responses to the challenge of Blackness represented by Malcolm X, the Nation of Islam, and the courageous young shock troops of the Student Nonviolent Coordinating Committee, as well as all the magnificent Black foreparents of his own familiar cultural and religious traditions; his deepening and expanding concern about the harsh realities of economic injustice in America and across the globe; his powerful determination to identify his life and his leadership with the cause of poor people of all colors; his audacious movement out of the more familiar settings of his native South into the uncertain, exploding cauldrons of the Northern cities; his increasingly strident denunciations of white American racism; his courageous willingness to carry on a religiously and politically motivated lover's quarrel with the leaders of his nation and with all of their followers who were destroying the peoples of Southeast Asia and the hopes of poor people in America; his call for the revolutionary transformation of our nation's institutions toward compassion; his attempt to gather the poor people of this country and organize them into a visionary nonviolent revolutionary force to challenge the status quo of economic injustice in America; his assassination in the midst of that unparalleled and utopian quest for a Poor People's Campaign—these and other manifestations of the post-

1963 life of our hero have generally been missing from our celebrations of his work.

In my attempts to challenge this American amnesia, I am driven not simply by a historian's concern to get the story right, or by a friend's and coworker's commitment to testify to what I saw and heard and felt in my ten years of friendship and companionship with Martin King. More important is my conviction that the King who wrestled with the shadows—both personal and national—is more valuable to us in the 1990s than the King of the unbroken sunshine, though of course, it was never *really* unbroken. For I am still convinced that Martin's friend, brother, and marching companion, Rabbi Abraham J. Heschel, was right when he said shortly before King's death that "the whole future of America depends upon the impact and influence of Dr. King."

We who must now continue to wrestle with the growing reality of economic injustice in America, we who are challenged to face the fact that this nation has no humane future if it does not deal with the re-humanizing of its cities, we who remember King's unceasing warnings about the triple American evils of racism, militarism, and materialism, are engaged and assisted much more fully by the King of the post-1963 years than by an earlier, more convenient hero. So the central concern of this work is ultimately one of healing, awakening, moving forward. My hope is that we might press ourselves beyond amnesia and engage the tougher, more difficult King. As with Malcolm, one of King's most significant characteristics in his last years was his willingness to take great risks on behalf of hope: to shake himself free of the more familiar, triumphant settings and to break loose toward the solitary unchartedness of the wilderness, especially if that exploratory movement might help him to respond more faithfully to the cries of the poor, the vulnerable, and the marginalized women, men, and children of our nation and our world.

Surely that capacity for creative exploration in search of a compassionate "more perfect union" is a critical need among us today. Perhaps, then, it is good that the national commission that was originally responsible for guiding and coordinating the King holiday celebrations has fallen prey to new more narrow agendas within the federal government and within the King family circles. Perhaps the memory of Martin King needs to be broken free from all official attempts to manage, market, and domesticate him. At this moment near the closing of his century, we need a truly free and inconvenient hero, one who may help us to explore new dimensions of our freedom, not simply as a private agenda, but to follow his unmanageable style of seeking and using freedom to serve the needs of the most vulnerable, the most unfree among us. My concern here is that we stop holding King captive to his most pliant history in order that he might help us to break free toward our most creative future as persons, as communities, as a nation. How else will we be worthy of such a magnificently inconvenient hero? How else will we discover the hero within us all?

MARTIN LUTHER KING

CHAPTER 1

THE INCONVENIENT HERO

The Last Years of Martin Luther King, Jr.

> Dead men make
> such convenient heroes: They
> cannot rise
> to challenge the images
> we would fashion from their lives.[1]
>
> Carl Wendell Himes, Jr.

It was in January 1979 that the first formal call was made for the nation to claim Martin Luther King, Jr., as its official hero. President Jimmy Carter, a fellow Georgian, used the occasion of King's fiftieth birthday to speak at Ebenezer Baptist Church, that familiar home base in Atlanta, to urge the establishment of a national holiday honoring Ebenezer's most famous child. In the course of his statement, Carter touched one of the keys to King's deepest meaning for the nation when he said that the martyred leader had "called out to the best in people.... He spoke of the America that had never been, of the America we hope will be."[2]

There were, of course, many interpretations of the nature of that "America we hope will be," and in the struggles that later took place within Congress and across the nation over the appropriateness of King as national hero, the tendency was to choose the most facile interpretation, the one that fit most readily with the America that is now and has been. Somehow, it seemed that

1

the furthest most Americans could go with King was to that magnificent day in August 1963, before the Lincoln Memorial, when he spoke of his "dream." (Of course, he also pointed that day to "the unspeakable horrors of police brutality" inflicted on black people, and said he refused to be satisfied "as long as the Negro's basic mobility is from a smaller ghetto to a larger one." But it was easier to deal with the dream of an America where black and white children would hold hands in unity.)[3]

As a result, in most of the celebrations of King's life which prepared the way for this month's inauguration of the official national holiday, the dominant image has been that of the great orator at the Mall, the dreamer of interracial harmony, the stirring and mildly challenging preacher. So, too, in the debates over the establishment of the federal holiday, the supporters appeared to feel a need to make Martin King as harmless as George Washington had become, to trim him to the measure of America in the 1970s and 1980s. Then, in one of the most ironic scenes of all, President Reagan, in November 1983, moving toward an election year, apparently forgetting his earlier facetious question about whether or not King might have been a communist, decided that he was really in support of the national holiday. But that could have been less than a favor, for when he signed the bill into law, Reagan continued the trivialization of the new hero's vision by offering his own homily on King's significance. He said,

> Traces of bigotry still mar America. So each year on Martin Luther King Day, let us not only recall Dr. King but rededicate ourselves to the commandments he believed in and sought to live every day: "Thou shalt love thy God with all thy heart and thou shall love thy neighbor as thyself."[4]

It was a strange embrace, especially coming from a man whose administration seemed determined to retreat to an imaginary America of the past, a man who had opposed all of the legislation

for which King had fought and died, and who was just then
exulting in the invasion of Grenada—an act King would surely
have passionately condemned. But the president was clearly
representative of vast numbers of the people (including the
people of Congress), totally ambiguous in their reception of the
new hero, uncomfortable with the idea of an "America that had
never been," wondering how they would absorb this second
"father" of our country, uncertain how to explain him to the children who would ask why the school was closed.

Perhaps this was the moment that the poet had anticipated
back in 1969 while the blood still stained the motel balcony,
while King had just begun the process of being transformed from
a troublesome, dangerous black presence to a candidate for
national hero. Carl Wendell Himes, Jr., saw what was coming and
wrote then,

> Now that he is safely dead
> Let us praise him
> build monuments to his glory
> sing hosannas to his name.
> Dead men make
> such convenient heroes: They
> cannot rise
> to challenge the images
> we would fashion from their lives
> And besides,
> it is easier to build monuments
> than to make a better world.
> So, now that he is safely dead
> we, with eased consciences
> will teach our children
> that he was a great man . . . knowing
> that the cause for which he lived
> is still a cause
> and the dream for which he died

is still a dream,
a dead man's dream.[5]

This trial by ordeal at the hands of a nation not yet ready for the demanding grandeur of its hero was poignantly placed in context for me not long ago in a college class filled with students who had all grown up since the death in Memphis. As we studied the post-1963 development of Martin King, one young man blurted out, "It's just not fair. I feel like all through these years of schooling and TV I've just been shut off from the last part of Dr. King's life." He paused, then added, "It's like all I can remember is that great 'I Have a Dream' speech, and then, it's as if he was shot right after that—you know, like the day after, and then the next thing I know is there's going to be a national holiday." He stopped again, and quietly asked, "Do you know what I mean?"[6]

I thought and felt that I knew what he meant, sensed that it was at least in part a *cri de coeur*, imploring, demanding that the door be opened, that he be introduced to the hero, that he be given the chance to struggle with the option of building monuments or building a better world—or both. Strangely enough, that student's imprecation sent me back to the pious words of President Reagan, and I wondered what it would be like, really to *re-call* Martin King, to evoke his life, his presence, his spirit, especially that part between the dream of Washington and the nightmare of Memphis.

Some months before he was killed, King had already begun that re-calling, that recollection, for himself and others. On Christmas Eve, 1967, he spoke to his congregation in Ebenezer and said,

> I must confess to you today that not long after talking about that dream [in Washington] I started seeing it turn into a nightmare. I remember the first time I saw that dream turn into a nightmare, just a few weeks after I had talked about it. It was when four beautiful, unoffending, innocent Negro girls were murdered in a church in Birmingham, Alabama.[7]

Martin Luther King pulls up a cross burned on the front lawn of his home in 1960.

Those words provide an essential key, not only for the students who seek to enter the post-March-on-Washington phase of King's life, but for all of us who are prepared to deal with what could well be called the second coming of Martin Luther King, Jr. For his greatness may rest not so much in the dream, but in his willingness to continue to hope, to struggle, to develop new vision, to call others to a new America, right in the midst of nightmares, despair, and brutally broken bodies. While the echoes of the explosives still reverberated in many hearts, King had to face the families, comfort the bereaved, recognize the fact that the church was bombed partly because it had been a focal point for Birmingham's community in the struggle he had led just months before. In the face of that nightmare he had to re-vision the dream.

Then, before the year had ended, death struck again in Dallas. This time the entire nation was touched, but King, and his family, had to deal with the special implications of Kennedy's assassination for him. For he was now living in a time when national white support for the movement toward justice and equality seemed to be wavering. King had to come to terms with the polls which said that the majority of white citizens believed that "the Negroes were pressing too hard, asking for too much," and he had to match them with the reality of the black community which was just gearing up to demand from the nation a far more serious commitment to justice and equality.[8] On a certain level he was in full agreement with James Baldwin who was calling for a nationwide civil disobedience campaign, saying,

> If we don't move now, literally move, sit down, stand, walk, don't go to work, don't pay the rent, if we don't do every-thing now in our power to change this country, this country will turn out to be in the position, let us say, of Spain, a country which is so tangled and so trapped and im-mobilized by its interior discussion that it can't do any-thing else.[9]

To re-call King with honesty is to re-live those times before the hot urban summers when he, too, warned the nation that it must either deal with the "long-deferred issue of second-class citizenship . . . now or we can drive a seething humanity to a desperation it tried, asked, and hoped to avoid."[10]

This was the King who was deeply influenced by the courageous and militant shock troops of the freedom Movement, the Student Nonviolent Coordinating Committee (SNCC). To recall him is of necessity to re-call them, for they helped radicalize him, helped keep him pressed against the hard and jagged edges of the struggle, in places like Mississippi, where in 1964 three of their volunteers had disappeared at the outset of an audacious assault on the heart of America's system of legal segregation, an assault which brought hundreds of volunteers to the state to share in what was known as Mississippi Summer. As everyone quickly realized, James Chaney, Michael Goodman, and Mickey Schwerner had not just disappeared, they were dead, even while King was visiting Neshoba County where their bodies were ultimately found. He had to endure those deaths, more deaths, nightmare deaths.[11]

In this time of his transformation King also had to live with the compromising role he played later that summer when Mississippi's martyr-full freedom movement sent some of its best representatives (who had come, as it were, "out of great tribulation") to challenge the unjust, undemocratic Democratic national convention of 1964. For when the Freedom Democrats, as they were called, brought their black-led interracial delegation to Atlantic City in August to challenge the all-white racist regulars from Mississippi, King was among the national leaders who urged the battle-weary freedom fighters to accept a compromise which would have allowed them only a token presence at the convention. Some of the SNCC folks never forgave Martin for that decision, believing that he had capitulated to his white, liberal establishment supporters who were tied to Lyndon Johnson's fierce bandwagon. Martin had to live with that. It was all part of his becoming.[12]

Shortly after Mississippi Summer, word came that King would be awarded the Nobel Peace Prize for his leadership of the nonviolent struggle for justice in the U.S.A. He took the honor and responsibility seriously, and on his way to Oslo in December he stopped in England long enough to condemn his own government and the British for refusing to take a strong stand against South Africa. In December 1964 King was clear on the need to "join in nonviolent action to bring freedom and justice to South Africa by a massive movement for economic sanctions." Did Ronald Reagan know that the hero he wanted to recall was one who had announced in 1964,

> There are dangers of civil war in South Africa. We have a unique responsibility, but our Governments have failed to act decisively. Why do our Governments refuse to intervene effectively now? Must they wait until there is a blood bath before they recognize the crisis?[13]

Can one who asks such questions ever be safely dead?

Two months later, in February 1965, our Nobel Peace Laureate was occupying an appropriate space—the Selma jail—when Malcolm X came down to visit, only weeks before his death. By then that other magnificent hero had begun his own second coming, had already become "much more than there was time for him to be." In Selma he told Coretta King that he was really an ally. And later Martin King could say, "It was tragic that Malcolm was killed, he was really coming around, moving away from racism. He had such a sweet spirit." To re-call Martin is to re-call Malcolm. They were complementary, and by the end of their lives, they knew it.[14]

What King knew as well was that the triumphant Selma to Montgomery march in the spring of 1965 had been paid for with the lives of black and white people, and that dozens of courageous persons had been badly beaten to win the right for thousands to march. Part of the noticeable deepening of the shadows in the leader's face in these last years was the recognition as well that the Selma march was not a new beginning but the end of an era. It was the last of the great, traditional Southern marches, with King as the undisputed (at least to public view) leader of the cause. It marked the climax of the long, hard, and costly struggle against legalized public segregation and struck a major blow for justice in the voting process. It was closing the least complicated period of the modern movement toward "the America we hope will be."

Meanwhile, the cause itself was being transformed, deepened, expanded, being made more complex—and so was King. An ever-expanding shadow named Vietnam had begun to fall over the hope, and the Nobel Laureate, the Christian minister, the humane lover of the poor, felt he had to speak publicly about what was going on, quietly, deferentially, cautiously at first. But even so tentative a mode was too bold for the president who was building toward nightmares overseas. United Nations Ambassador Arthur Goldberg was assigned to assure King that all was well, that peace "was in the air," and Martin later said he was stunned by the nature and amount of the pressure that was mounted against those first public statements he made on the way. "They told me I wasn't an expert in foreign affairs, and they were all experts," he said. They told him, "I knew only civil rights and I should stick to that." King backed down, temporarily, but the die had been cast. The Negro hero had been told to stay in his place, colored place, to leave foreign affairs to white folks, to squelch any naive thoughts that nonviolence in Birmingham might be in any way related to nonviolence in Vietnam.[15]

But King could not be tied down anywhere. That was part of his strange appeal, and great danger. Increasingly he came to see himself as advocate for the poor and the oppressed wherever they were. They became like a fire in his bones. (To re-call him is to re-call them.) So he could not ignore Watts when it exploded in August 1965, nor could he put up with all the facile official explanations and rationalizations, all the condemnations and evasions. He had seen the seething, felt it, heard it, predicted its rising explosive force. When he walked through Watts and saw the faces of the young men, he knew them, recognized they were his children, understood the desperation that led them to stand amidst the charred remains of their community and say, "We won, because we made the whole world pay attention to us."[16]

Much of the rest of his life, brief life, was given to searching out a way to respond to the men-children and their sisters, and the harshness of their experience, to catch the meaning of the explosions in Watts and in all the urban rebellions which would write their incendiary message across the land: "Pay attention!" So he moved, demanding of us that we look directly into the eye of the storm, face the nightmarish deterioration of Northern black urban life, recognize its experiences of economic exploitation, joblessness, and underemployment, neglected schools, and overpriced, absentee-landlord housing, with no one seeming to care, to hear—until the fires raged. To re-call him is to feel the fire smoldering.

When he faced the nation after Watts, calling for the attention which the fires were seeking, his language was sharper, harsher than it had ever been before. That fall he wrote,

> In my travels in the North I was increasingly becoming disillusioned with the power structures there. I encountered the tragic and stubborn fact that in virtually no major city was there a mayor possessing statesmanship, understanding, or even strong compassion on the civil rights questions.... All my experience indicated that hope of voluntary understanding was chimerical; there was blindness, obtuseness, and rigidity that would only be altered by a dynamic movement.[17]

Watts finally convinced him. It was time, King said, for the freedom movement to go North, where he predicted "a sharpened conflict will unfold."[18]

Driven by the faces of the young men in Los Angeles, by the fire in his heart, by the obsession with the need to create a more militant, Northern-honed version of nonviolent struggle for justice, King moved into one of Chicago's poorest, most exploited, black communities. The move was partly symbolic, but nevertheless posed a challenge to all who would now re-call him, to recognize that his love of neighbor demanded that he be neighbor, that he insert his life into the condition of the neighbor, that he challenge, as he used to say, "the whole structure of Jericho Road," that he do it with his total being.[19]

And yet there was always something tearing, dividing him, preventing the unrelenting focus. In 1966, as he turned his face to Chicago, the South would not be denied its own continuing fire. Late that spring the quixotic, courageous James Meredith had drawn it down upon himself on a Mississippi road, shot down (but not seriously wounded) just as he set out on a one-man "March against Fear" through his native state. As King met in Memphis with other civil rights leaders, first around Meredith's bed, then in long, harsh gatherings preparing to continue the march, it was clear that there was no more business as usual for them. They could not escape the fires they had helped to create. The older movement no longer existed. The power of blackness was now on the agenda. The role of whites had become a subject of rancorous debate, and all the way down Highway 51, cutting through the heart of Mississippi, facing the still-untamed official violence of the state, the debate went on, and the cry of "Black Power," brought international attention to what was already taking place—the transformation of the Southern freedom movement, the ending of the era that had begun in Montgomery, Alabama, in 1955. A generation of social change had been jammed into little more than a decade. Explosions were inevitable. Besides, in spite of all its confusion and disarray, the Meredith march—building on the life and death of many earlier freedom workers—had witnessed powerful expressions of black courage and determination in places where fear had reigned less than five years ago. Now, for instance, in the face of tear gas, whips, sticks, and gun butts, a local black woman participating in the march could stand up in the mud and say, "We are not going to stay ignorant, and backward, and scared." The rock had surely been cracked, and King's presence was a part of it. (To re-call him, is to recall what it costs to crack rocks in America.)[20]

Chastened, shaken, enlightened, but not fundamentally discouraged or put off by the surge of Blackness represented by Stokely Carmichael, Floyd McKissick and the younger forces of SNCC and the Congress of Racial Equality (CORE), King returned North in 1966 as the fires of summer were beginning to mount again. Distressed but not surprised by the lethargic response of the federal government to the official violence of Mississippi, Martin prepared to do battle with the most formidable political machine in the nation, Mayor Richard Daley's Democratic Party of Chicago. Under the best of circumstances, King needed at least two years of organizing, training, experimenting, failing, and learning how to take on this new reality. He was off his home base, operating in a different milieu, up against not only the epitome of "blindness, obtuseness, and rigidity," but facing a highly skilled political operative who had coopted a significant segment of black political leadership into his camp, and who had the money and the troops and the knowledge of the local terrain that King could only develop over time.

But the fire-seared hero was not given two years. So he seized the time that he had. Out of the tangled skein of life and political corruption in the most segregated city of the North, the Southern Christian Leadership Conference (SCLC) forces and their Chicago allies chose to attack the problem of racially segregated housing. He had dreamed of mobilizing tens of thousands of mostly black people in Chicago to carry out acts of massive civil disobedience to press the city's political and economic leadership to the bargaining tables. But the realities of the hastily organized activities that summer were very different. After a July 10th Freedom Sunday march by some forty thousand persons to witness King tacking up demands on the door of city hall, the largest direct action mobilization after that brought somewhat fewer than a thousand marchers into the dangerous precincts of Marquette Park, one of the many segregated, antiblack communities of Chicago. It was here that the demonstrators met fierce opposition, needed all the protection that Daley's police force could provide, and went through the frightening experience of having Martin King hit by a rock. When it was over King said,

> I've never seen anything like it. . . . I've been in many demonstrations all across the South, but I can say that I have never seen—even in Mississippi and Alabama—mobs as hostile and as hate-filled as I've seen in Chicago.[21]

When it was over, King knew it really wasn't. Threats of even more dangerous SCLC-led confrontations with the fears and hatred of Chicago's white neighborhoods pushed Daley and his forces to the bargaining table, but not a great deal was gained there, and it was not over, only beginning. Fifteen years later, with a black mayor sitting in Daley's chair (but not taking his place), it was not really over, and the danger of re-calling King is that the questions of "Who is my neighbor?" and "What does love demand?" are still waiting on our answers.

For King, the answers were constantly expanding and deepening, raking him through fire, pressing him on to more and more exposed and dangerous ground—like Vietnam. Resisting both the threats and the blandishments of the war-obsessed president, recognizing the scurrilous, blackmailing ammunition that his own personal weaknesses had provided to the eavesdropping FBI, King refused to back away from his opposition to the brutal war against the Vietnamese. For him, the faces of the burning children and the self-immolated monks were extensions of the faces he had seen in Watts. The forms of the American soldiers, so terribly still in body bags, so emotionally crippled by the crimes against God and humanity they were forced to commit, were too often mirror images of his neighbors in Chicago. (Somehow, he seemed to know instinctively what presidents—and we who follow them—refuse to learn: nothing in "the commandments he believed in" set any national boundaries around the neighbors he was called to love. And nothing in the life of that Jesus, who Mr. Reagan was indirectly quoting, provided any indication that it was possible to love neighbors while also burning them, bombing them, targeting them for missiles, or undermining their search for revolutionary, life-affirming change—even Marxist-led change.)

For this man who was neighbor to the world, who was brother to the poor, who was an unsparing, relentlessly honest lover of the nation, it was impossible to be silent on Vietnam. Black people told him to be still, for his voice would anger the giver of all perfect gifts in the White House. White people told him to be still because he was not qualified to speak to issues that they had been in charge of for so many destructive years. Members of his own organization warned him about what his opposition to the war would do to cut down on financial contributions from their friends who saw no connection between Mississippi and the Mekong Delta (it was not yet popular for liberals to oppose the war). King, who felt the connection like fire in his heart, finally moved against all this advice and stood up in Riverside Church in New York City, precisely one year to the day before his assassination, and let the nation and the world know who he was in those days of nightmares and visions and what he thought were the political implications of his religious beliefs.[22]

Did Governor Reagan of California hear him in 1967? Is this the same Martin Luther King, Jr., he wants us now to recall, to re-call, who said,

> My ministry is in obedience to the one who loved his enemies so fully that he died for them. What then can I say to the Vietcong or to Castro or to Mao as a faithful minister of this one? Can I threaten them with death or must I not share with them my life?

Who dares recall this man who defined the essence of his identity, "beyond the calling of race or nation or creed" as a child of the living God and sought to live by that definition, saying, "I believe that the Father is deeply concerned especially for his suffering and helpless and outcast children [and] I come tonight to speak for them." To recall him is to rethink our categories of nationalism, patriotism, and national security. For here is a national hero who loved his country, and who claimed that speaking for the suffering people of every nation was,

> the privilege and burden of all of us who deem ourselves bound by allegiances and loyalties which are broader and deeper than nationalism and which go beyond our nation's self-defined goals and positions.

Here is a hero who declares that love of God and love of neighbor mean that,

> we are called to speak for the weak, for the voiceless, for victims of our nation and for those it calls enemy; for no document from human hands can make these humans any less our brother.

In 1967, this hero, who was then, in the eyes of many persons, not hero, but "communist dupe," "trouble-maker," "traitor," or at best "naive"—this very live man stood in Riverside Church, called our country "the greatest purveyor of violence in the world today," and pleaded with us, because he loved us, to stop bombing the people of Vietnam, to take the initiative in the peace-making process, for the sake of the Vietnamese, for the sake of our children, for the sake of God. Beyond Vietnam, he urged us away from our deeply etched racism, militarism, materialism, from our flaccid acceptance of "structural unemployment" in our nation, from our "morbid fear of communism." All of these, he said, had put us on "the wrong side" of the poor people's revolutions across the world, and he challenged us, for our good and theirs, to stand with the poor, at home and abroad. According to King,

> Our only hope . . . lies in our ability to recapture the revolutionary spirit [of America] and go out into a sometimes

hostile world declaring eternal hostility to poverty, racism, and militarism.

With that speech, and others like it, King became the major national spokesperson for a morally based stand against the war, inspiring the burgeoning antiwar movement, calling upon the younger people of the nation to refuse to participate, urging them, and their ministers, to declare themselves conscientious objectors to military service—based on love of God and of neighbor, based on obedience to the Prince of Peace.[23] With that speech, the rage of the White House and the FBI and other related institutions became more virulent. With that speech, the rifle sights became more sharply focused than ever before. (Those who are serious about re-calling King must therefore be serious, too, about the risks of his company, his unexpurgated company.)

Meanwhile, the fires would not abate—in Vietnam, in the American cities, in Martin King's bones. Indeed, they increased in force and power. In the summer of 1967 scores of America's urban areas were enveloped by the leaping flames of a series of rebellions which seemed at the time to move the nation to the very edges of racial warfare. Nearly 150 cities were involved, but the intensity of the struggles was focused in July of that year on Newark, New Jersey, and on Detroit.[24] In the Motor City, symbol of the nation's great technological prowess, the message of its great moral failures was broadcast to the world, as five thousand American paratroopers were called in (some already veterans of the other battleground, in Southeast Asia), with helicopters sweeping the skies and armored vehicles patrolling the streets, and the death toll—almost all black—rising above forty.

Earlier that spring, a sensitive reporter who traveled with King for ten days had seen the fires in him, had understood their connection to the burning of the cities and the rice fields. David Halberstam wrote, "King has decided to represent the ghettos; he will work in them and speak for them." Then the writer added a significant comment for all who seek to re-call:

But their voice is harsh and alienated. If King is to speak for them truly, then his voice must reflect theirs; it, too, must be alienated and it is likely to be increasingly at odds with the rest of American society.[25]

Apparently, love of God and neighbor—God in Vietnam, God under fire in Detroit—required nonconformity, conflict, confrontation with "the rest of American society." Thus, it was not surprising that this hero who chose the burning communities of the poor as his base should take umbrage with a president whose response to the burnings was to scold and threaten the black people who were calling attention to their pain and their powerlessness. Nor was it strange that King should forthrightly condemn a Congress which seemed totally unresponsive to the need for serious, socially concerned legislation.

On the day after Johnson sent the troops and tanks into Detroit, King sent the president a telegram, saying,

> The suicidal and irrational acts which plague our streets daily are being sowed and watered by the irrational and equally suicidal debate and delay in Congress. This is an example of moral degradation.[26]

Later, King let the fire continue to speak from within him, angrily asking,

> How can the administration with quivering anger denounce the violence of ghetto Negroes when it has given an example of violence in Asia that shocks the world? ... Only those who are fighting for peace have the moral authority to lecture on nonviolence.[27]

Then, noting that even after the urban fires had begun to die down, and the troops pulled out, the leadership of the federal government offered nothing in the way of solutions save another study commission and a call for a day of prayer, King pressed on.

He did not play with such matters, especially in the time of the fires. "As a minister," he said, "I take prayer too seriously to use it as an excuse for avoiding work and responsibility." He concluded that "when a government commands more wealth and power than has ever been known in the history of the world, and offers no more than this, it is worse than blind. It is provocative." Publicly, Lyndon Johnson ignored King's calls from within the fire zone. Privately, the anger continued to build against this black man who dared challenge the nation's leadership on such high moral grounds.

The fire within was driving the hero far from the America which existed, deep into the heart of his smoldering children's alienation, pressing him to work even more fiercely toward "the America we hope will be." It was a harsh and difficult journey. All through the second half of 1967 King was tentatively, often vaguely, outlining its movement. Central to his vision was the possibility of developing a major, national nonviolent movement which would call on the fires in the hearts of the young men and women who were now the victims of America, a movement which would "transmute the deep rage of the ghetto into a constructive and creative force." Sometimes he used the language of an earlier, Gandhian contribution and referred to what he envisioned as a "nonviolent army." Whatever its name, King said what was necessary was a movement which would "cripple the operation of an oppressive society" until it was ready to listen to the cries and see the real fires of the poor.

By the end of the year, the vision was becoming consistent with King's fundamental sense of the need for a multiracial force of the poor. He said,

> The dispossessed of this nation—the poor, both white and Negro—live in a cruelly unjust society. They must organize a revolution against that injustice, not against the lives of . . . their fellow citizens, but against the structures through which the society is refusing to take means . . . to lift the load of poverty.[28]

The fires at home, abroad, within, were pressing him toward the edges. Now, in the last months of his life, the man who had depended for so long on the help and cooperation of an essentially friendly federal government was facing what may have been the harshest of all realities. "The government," he said, "is preoccupied with war and is determined to husband every resource for military adventures rather than social transformation." This led him to the only possible conclusion for someone on the fiery, tearful, joyous pathway to an America that did not yet exist. King said,

> Negroes must, therefore, not only formulate a program; they must fashion new tactics which do not count on government good will, but serve, instead, to compel unwilling authorities to yield to the mandates of justice.[29]

The nightmarish time between dream and vision was now possessing Martin Luther King. He had begun to face the fact that he would have to organize confrontative, revolutionary, nonviolent opposition to his own government in order to move toward a new, compassionate America. There were no blue-prints or road maps. There were relatively few companions who were ready to live and die in search of so unknown a way. But King pressed on.

In December 1967, standing between dream and vision, refusing to be overcome by the necessary nightmare of that position, King said,

> Nonviolent protest must now mature to a new level to correspond to heightened black impatience and stiffened white resistance. This higher level is mass civil disobedience. There must be more than a statement to the larger society, there must be a force that interrupts its functioning at some key point. That interruption must not, however, be clandestine or surreptitious. It must be open and, above all, conducted by large masses without violence. If the jails are filled to thwart it, its meaning will become even clearer.[30]

Although often overtaken by doubts, distractions, and fears, King pressed on, clarifying for himself and for others the shape of the coming Poor People's Campaign. (All who seek to re-call the Campaign as King had begun to envision it will need to move beyond the rain-soaked, often dispirited symbolic actions of Resurrection City in the late spring of 1968, and see the fiery annealing of dream, nightmare, and vision in this man who had made a "preferential option for the poor" before that term was coined. All those who seek to re-call him in authenticity must then decide where they/we stand in this time between dream and vision, between the America that never has been yet and that which must be—for the safety of the world.) He continued to work with it, play with it, run from its implications, and then return to deepen its possibilities:

> The Negro revolt is evolving into more than a quest for desegregation and equality. It is a challenge to a system that has created miracles of production and technology to create justice. If humanism is locked outside the system, Negroes will have revealed its inner core of despotism and a far greater struggle for liberation will unfold.[31]

Just a few weeks before the bullet struck (helping to explain to the children, and to us, whose bullet it was and why it was fired), King took his own sense of the American dilemma and challenge even further. By then he had come to the conclusion that the black freedom struggle was actually "exposing the evils that are deeply rooted in the whole structure of our society. It reveals systemic rather than superficial flaws and suggests that radical reconstruction of society itself is the real issue to be faced."[32]

Finally, continuing to see the world whole, to recognize all the sisters and brothers, whatever their disguise, King placed the evolving black struggle that he was even then re-dreaming, re-visioning, into the context of God's larger world, and declared with great power and conviction:

The storm is rising against the privileged minority of the earth, from which there is no shelter in isolation or armament. The storm will not abate until a just distribution of the fruits of the earth enables men everywhere to live in dignity and human decency. The American Negro ... may be the vanguard of a prolonged struggle that may change the shape of the world, as billions of deprived shake and transform the earth in the quest for life, freedom and justice.[33]

Who dares re-call this man, when all the plagues he fought are still among us, standing in the way of "the America we hope to be": poverty and exploitation, racism, militarism, materialism, manipulated anticommunism? How shall we re-call him when the America which has been is still protected and justified by Bible-quoting presidents and supine legislators who offer no visionary leadership to a spiritually crippled people?

Who dare rededicate themselves to the causes of this hero? Who is there now, when major portions of his black middle class have made their peace, found equal opportunity in the America that is? Someone.

Who is there now, when the overwhelming experience of the black church is still focused on an individualistic religious experience, breaking faith with the Tubmans, the Turners, the Truths, and the Kings (and *the* King?) Someone.

Who is there now when so many of the black youth in whom the fire once burned are now being cooled out by drugs, by jail, by military lies, by poisoned cultural opium in music and on screens, by big money for playing small games? Someone.

Who is there when so many of his white comrades now stand back in cynicism, fear, success, and puzzlement? Someone.

Who is there when so many of the poor (and recently poor) now compete for crumbs across racial and ethnic lines, rather than standing together to vision, to pray, to re-collect, to plan, to struggle? Someone.

Who stands with a hero who insists on living for the broken and exploited, who refuses to deny nightmares, who will not let dreams die, and is not afraid to go on exploring, stumbling, trembling, wherever visions lead him? Someone.

Who will open the door for the children, to let them see him, feel him, as he was, to re-call him as he is, perhaps to expose their hungry, directionless lives to the flaming vector of his passion for the poor? Someone.

Is he safely dead? Perhaps we should re-call him and see. Now. Perhaps in the process we may learn again how to live—unsafely, in love with God and neighbor, with cleansing, purifying fire, with the America that is yet to be created—by us. Perhaps if we re-call him at this level even presidents will understand what Rabbi Abraham Heschel meant when he spoke to a group of his co-religionists ten days before King's death and said,

> Martin Luther King, Jr., is a voice, a vision, and a way. I call upon every Jew to harken to his voice, to share his vision, to follow in his way. The whole future of America will depend on the impact and influence of Dr. King.[34]

Surely, neither the Rabbi nor the nonconforming hero will object if we add every other name we choose (including our own) after the name of those to whom Dr. Heschel specifically directed his challenge. For it may be only as we add our names, our intentions, our lives, personally, collectively to the list of re-callers that we shall find out if the hero, or we heroes, shall live, shall rise, shall open doors for our children, beyond George Washington, toward a new, rough-hewn father of the country still being born.

CHAPTER 2

GETTING READY
FOR THE HERO

he-ro. 1. In mythology and legend, a person, often born of one mortal and one divine parent, who is endowed with great courage and strength, celebrated for bold exploits, and favored by the gods. 2. Anyone noted for feats of courage or nobility of purpose; especially one who has risked or sacrificed his or her life.

American Heritage Dictionary of the English Language (1970)

Somewhere in the midst of the endless wisdom of the Buddhists this encouraging, disciplining promise stands forth: "When the student is ready, the teacher will appear." For years these simple words and their profound message have been a source of great hope for me, a way to deal with much unreadiness, an opening to many appearings. Then, late last fall, the promise returned in another form and spoke to me as I wrestled with the possible meanings of the imminent appearance of my friend Martin Luther King, Jr., in the pantheon of our nation's official heroes.

Playing with the ancient wisdom, preparing for January 20, 1986, remembering his public lifetime—thirteen explosive years that became a generation of transformation—two variations on the Buddhist theme emerge: "When the nation is ready, the hero will appear." Or, equally appealing to me: "When the hero is ready, the nation will appear." Taking off from such meandering thoughts, the wondering/wandering began, moving across the serrated surface of our wounded, immature, and dangerous

23

nation, probing into the painful, magnificent depths of our broken, beautiful country, my country, Martin's country, still-being-born country.

It may just be, brother, as the old folks used to sing, "We didn't know who you were." Or did we? And did we also know that we really weren't ready for any hero like you, and decided that instead of getting ready, we'd get comfortable?

Of course, some of us tried to get ready for a while, finding a taste of Birmingham and Greenwood and Selma and even a bit of "Black Power, Baby!" to be exciting; but Chicago and Cleveland and Harlem and Detroit and Watts and everywhere North and Black and urban, and everywhere poor, unrepresented, exploited, and unemployed, and all the unpronounceable Asian places where women and children and "gooks" were being burned—and all that unromantic, un-American, unglamorous, untelevised, untidy, unsafe, unclear, un-Southern, unpaid-for organizing stuff was just too much for us.

Could it be that some of us did suspect who you were but decided that we first needed to get our piece of the pie, of the rock, of the action—of whatever it is that pieces come off/in?

So it looks like you appeared before we were ready, Brother Martin, and threw us off balance, and we tried to hold on to rocks and pies and sweet, gentle, unchallenging Jesus. Is it too late to get ready? Or should we just smooth you off, and cut you down, and fit you with blinders, and quiet your sound, so that you can crawl into our gilded prison, and be a hero who won't run around with gods—or God?

"When the hero is ready. . . ." Were you ready, Martin, to be the hero with a thousand faces for us? Pastor and political leader; seeker and teacher; Moses and Messiah; mystic and mobilizer; husband and lonely traveler; father and world deliverer; child of the black church and satisfier of all the spiritual hunger endemic to white America; adviser to presidents and friend of the unkempt poor; Martin-of-the-March-on-Washington, eloquent, apparently undemanding dreamer, and

Martin-after-the-child-killing-bombings, after the Mississippi murders, after the assassination of beautiful Malcolm, after the funerals for Jimmy Jackson, for James Reeb, for Viola Luizzo, after-Harlem-Martin, after Watts, after Chicago, after Detroit, after Newark, after the flames engulfing monks and naked children in Vietnam? After nightmares?

Were you ready, brother, even though you knew it was coming, for the criticism from black folks, from deep in the ancestral community? Were you ready for those of us who didn't want to upset the tantrum-tending president, who didn't want to be uncomfortable just when things were beginning to look good—for us—who didn't want to lose our jobs, who were aching for the rock, the pie, the action, the mainstream? Were you ready for all of us who turned back when you started holding hands with the poor, with the peacemakers, with the Vietnamese "enemies"? Were you ready for all of us who sang the old refrain, "It's bad enough to be Black without being Red, too"? Dear Martin, dear hero, were you ready for all that pain?

And what about all the other folks "of good will" who were eager to set the white South straight, to use troops if necessary to show those "rednecks" what this country is all about—they said—but who didn't think there were any such problems in *their* community, North and white, and comfortable, and far from all those people whose hands you insisted on holding, and who might just have to get the troops on you if you got out of hand—in the North? Were you ready when they stopped holding and singing and giving and backed away and wondered out loud if you were qualified (meaning ready) to discuss foreign policy and national budgets and militarism and institutional racism and all the things only qualified white experts (and crazy "militant" people) talked about? Does it still hurt in the place where they/we backed off and left you exposed to the coming of the night?

Sometimes I wonder, can you tell us now who was it working in you in those last years, Martin? To get you talking like that and holding hands like that, daring to feel, trying to express the anger, the anguish and the stumbling words of the poor, all the poor, everywhere, standing up to presidents, FBI directors, wealthy donors, and death-dealing military and corporate systems like that, calling for new systems and values, acting like you really meant it when you sang the song, "Ain't gonna let NOBODY turn me round, keep on walking, keep on talking, marching up to freedom land." Was it old Dr. Du Bois? Luthuli? Lumumba? Gandhi? Claudia Jones? Or just Malcolm sneaking back around and doing it to you, to us? Or could it be that heroes' Daddys and Mommas do play with gods—or God? If so, then maybe the ashes in Atlanta, and everywhere, are still getting themselves ready for your rising, Martin "Phoenix" King. Are you ready? Are we? Are you getting ready? Are we?

While playing, praying, weeping, and laughing through such clearly un-Buddhist thoughts, I came across a slim volume of poetry titled *Drum Major for a Dream*.[1] Published in India, it consists of a group of poems by black and white North American authors, expressing their responses to the assassination of Martin King—before he was proclaimed hero. The poets ranged in age from schoolchildren to a retired minister, and their work varied much in quality. But almost all were written within the immediate period of King's death and bear an authenticity based on their fundamental honesty and intentionality.

The key which opened them to my wrestling with the National Hero and with his country was found in the words of Gwendolyn Brooks, that magnificent black mother artist, in the last poem in the book. She said of Martin,

> A man went forth with gifts.
> He was a prose poem.
> He was a tragic grace.
> He was a warm music.
> He tried to heal the vivid volcanoes.
> His ashes are
> > reading the world.

And in her verses on the living prose poem, on the grace, on the music, she opened up to me permission to inhabit the poetry, to dance in the songs, in the grace of the gods, in the amazing grace of God, and allowed me to stand in volcanic ash and sing. She offered—thank you, Sister Gwen—a possible way to see my friend, the hero, and his nation, our nation, again. So I entered this book of poems and let them pierce me and recognized that though they speak of death, none of them is the end of a conversation.

Indeed, they are now my companions on the endless journey to January 20, 1986, and I share my responses to them simply as an invitation to others, many others—black, white, brown, all others—to join the conversation, bring improvisations to the song, song of death, song of life, getting ready.

Carl Wendell Himes, Jr., was in his late twenties when the bullet came, expected, yet never quite prepared for. And he wrote his sorrow in the words:

> Now that he is safely dead
> Let us praise him
>   build monuments to his glory
>   sing hosannas to his name.
>   Dead men make
> such convenient heroes: They
>   cannot rise
>   to challenge the images
>   we would fashion from their lives
>   And besides,
> it is easier to build monuments
>   than to make a better world.
>   So, now that he is safely dead
> we, with eased consciences
>   will teach our children
>   that he was a great man . . . knowing
>   that the cause for which he lived

> is still a cause
>> and the dream for which he died
>>> is still a dream,
> a dead man's dream.

Safely? This man who was called by the FBI "the most danger-ous Negro . . . in this nation"? When will he be safely dead? Listen for him in January. Feel the tremors beneath the monuments. Hear the voices from the black past (and future) singing, beyond "Hosannas," singing with Martin, for Martin, "Ain't no grave can hold my body down."

Perhaps the youngest children will hear best, will receive the voices and the songs through ears and hearts not yet filled with the "Top Forty," through eyes that see beyond MTV and other diversions from getting ready. Perhaps they will sense that great men and women do not really die. Perhaps they will ask about his dream, his cause, suspecting that he lives, somewhere, nearby. Perhaps we will have the wisdom, the knowledge, and the courage to introduce them to the hero who, by the end of his life, was totally committed to the cause of the poor—in Mississippi, in Chicago, in Appalachia, in Vietnam, in Central America, in South Africa, in Memphis.

Perhaps we will tell them that the older dream, the famous, easier-to-handle dream, the forever-quoted dream of 1963 was no longer sufficient for him. Let them know that at the end, when the bullet finally came, he was dreaming of marching on Washington again, but this time to stay there, not just for speeches and for singing, but for audacious, challenging, divinely obedient action—to engage in a campaign of massive civil disobe-dience to try to stop the functioning of the national government. Tell them he planned to do this, calling on thousands and hundreds of thousands of lovers of justice until the cause of the poor became the nation's first priority, until all people were guar-anteed jobs or honest income, until our nation stopped killing Asians abroad and turned to tend to the desperate needs of its people at home.

Tell them that was the last dream. Then perhaps they will understand the bullet, why it came, from whom it came, and why neither the dream nor the dreamer can die in places where women and men and children give themselves to the building of "a better world" as the best monument to the hero. Wasn't that what our unsafe, lively brother kept saying toward the end: ". . . let us re-dedicate ourselves to the long and bitter—but beautiful—struggle for a new world." Tell the children. Invite them to walk with the hero, with us, in the cause, in the dream, building, always building.

Facing ourselves, facing the hero, we listen, developing one of the disciplines of those who are getting ready. We listen to Edith Lovejoy Pierce—and more:

> Above the shouts and the shots,
> The roaring flames and the siren's blare,
> Listen for the stilled voice of the man
> Who is no longer there.
>
> Above the tramping of the endless line
> Of marchers along the street,
> Listen for the silent step
> Of the dead man's invisible feet.
>
> Lock doors, put troops at the gate,
> Guard the legislative halls,
> But tremble when the dead man comes,
> Whose spirit walks through walls.

Maybe he's still getting ready, too. Maybe that overwhelming sadness in Washington, D.C., in the sodden spring of 1968, that attempt to carry forward Martin's last great, incomplete dream in the face of endless rain and despair and fear and massive disarray, was only the prelude to the coming Poor People's Campaign. In a nation with more than forty million persons existing below the poverty level today; with thousands of men and women sleeping

U.P.I.

King and Ralph Abernathy, June 1964, in a Florida jail after a sit-in at a segregated restaurant.

on the streets of our cities today (trillions of wasted military dollars later); with millions of unemployed and underemployed and no prospects in sight for real humanizing work for an entire generation of young people today (thousands of promises later)—it may be that the rising and the walking of the poor are still to come. It may be that only assassins and their keepers have really heard Martin's words from many years ago: "The dispossessed of this nation—the poor, both white and Negro—live in a cruelly unjust society. They must organize a revolution against that injustice, not against the lives of . . . their fellow citizens, but against the structures through which the society is refusing to . . . lift the load of poverty."

Listen. That was the voice of our hero in the last year of his life. That was his revolutionary spirit on behalf of the poor, on behalf of the nation. Are we ready for him? Can that living spirit really walk through walls? Walk through walls? Walk through walls! Like the barricades of our fears, the insistent shelters of our self-centeredness, the barriers of our great need for respectability, security, and safety?

Such walls! Powerful, surrounding us, devouring us, crushing us, filling us, each, all. Can you walk through, Martin? Are you ready? Am I? Are we? "Oh, sometimes it causes me to tremble. . . ."

When the hero appears, will we be ready for the walls to fall?

Sometimes the poet's voice is louder than dear Edith Pierce's measured, church-hymn tones. Another woman, Ruth Howard, coming from another place, shouts from the pages to us (the way Martin could shout, and *almost* get down into his back-home, Baptist, revival-preacher thing):

> O nation of greatness
>   And of fools—
> Hearken, hypocrites
> Who mock democracy:
>   You are as guilty
>   As that gutless coward
>   Who held the gun.

Martin Luther King:
>   Symbol of peace and love,
>   Voice of human rights and justice.
You could not silence him
Behind prison walls,
By obscene threats—
So you fashioned the bullet.
Dug the grave—
The voice is stilled.
>   But you will hear him,
>   For he will live in those
>   Who loved this man—
A man whose valor
Outshone an army of heroes.

Getting ready is letting the shouts, the accusations, the condemnations cascade over us, enter deep, breaking through the
walls, getting under the skin, flaming up the cool. Getting ready,
for some of us, is especially hard sometimes, for sometimes it is
being black and understanding that poetry is timeless. It is facing
the possibility that now, years later, years of "progress" and "equal
opportunity" and getting our piece, and swimming in the main
one, and sitting paralyzed in front of television for hours at a
stretch every impressionable childhood day—that now the
screaming, revival-time words might be not just for white folks,
but also for us, *for us*, to warn us of how fearful we are now, today
(so many years after the Memphis balcony). How terrified, how
guarded we have become against all that Martin King was called
then in his last, beleaguered years: "agitator," "trouble-maker,"
"radical," "communist sympathizer," "fanatic," "unpatriotic," "un-
American," "naive," "dangerous" to the status quo.

Do we dare fantasize about what we would do now, if he came
to our black-administered city, to challenge our leaders; if he
tried to question our values, and our bank accounts, and our
political machine; if he dared to undermine the morale and
question the Christian faith of our soldiers, of our officers, of our

chaplains—as they landed in Grenada, as they poised themselves on the borders of Nicaragua, as they enjoyed equality of opportunity to press the buttons of nuclear destruction, as they prepared for possible duty fighting "the communists" on behalf of the government of South Africa?

Are we, too, now frightened by people who organize unkempt and unrespectable folks to struggle for peace and justice here and abroad, who now take risks to do for escaping Central Americans what the Underground Railroad did for us—while we stand back, as far back as possible? Are we, too, now frightened in our respectable blackness by all the strange folks who, with King, really believe the way of love is more faithful to Jesus of Nazareth than the well-paid "defense" occupations of war-making, war-thinking, war-threatening, and death? Do we, too, mock democracy each time we back away, each time we fail to participate actively in the struggles for the transformation of our institutions and of this nation, in the defense of the poor, in the protection of the environment, in the questioning of our political leaders, in the teaching of ourselves and our children who the hero really was—and who he, and we, may yet become?

Can we still hear him? "Beautiful voice," we said. But did we hear what he was saying as the bullet smashed its way to our heart? Listening is getting ready. Has he penetrated beyond the messages of the mainstream, into our piece of the rock, to let us know that he was killed because he loved us, because he wanted us to discover our greatness, wanted us to seek the task of working for human rights and justice as more crucial than our private agendas of "making it"?

If we listen, we may well hear him. Right at the beginning, back in Montgomery time he dreamed us a great dream when he said to us, "If you will protest courageously, and with dignity and Christian love, when the history books are written in future generations, the historians will have to pause and say, 'There lived a great people—a black people—who injected new meaning and dignity into the veins of civilization.' This is our challenge and our overwhelming responsibility."

He was twenty-six years old when he saw that, said that, at the very first meeting of the Montgomery bus boycott forces. What a vision for that child/man! Seeing black folks, the stones the builders had rejected, seeing us, not floating contentedly in the mainstream, but challenging, standing, speaking, acting in such a way that new life, new meaning, new dignity are brought to an entire civilization? Oh Martin, did you mean it? Did you really love us so?

Are we ready? What will it mean to become our best selves, his best dream, "an army of heroes" for peace, for healing, for justice, for the poor, for life-giving rather than life-taking? Does it begin to feel good yet?

When the people are ready.... Did we think being black meant automatically being ready for the hero? Did we forget that we now know how to build and maintain prisons, to fashion bullets and missiles and bombs and dig the graves of the human race? Lord, what would Sojourner and Harriet think about such equal opportunity for death? Maybe, just maybe, they'll help their young brother Martin walk through our walls. Help him, sisters. Help us.

> Getting ready, getting ready
> > for the King's walk through.
> Sometimes,
> Sometimes,
> > It causes me to tremble.
> > What about you?

And who knows how much time we have to deal with the trembling walls—white walls, black walls, brown walls, fear walls, respectability walls, personal and national security walls, "my country-right-or-wrong" walls. Who knows? Poet Frank Carmody said:

> We have too little time to mourn the dead
> Bandage black around our hearts and
> > arms

Less time yet to build a dream
Of what the living might become.

No matter what the time, we take it, use it, and see the dream. It was grand, it was magnificent, constantly expanding, enlarging his heart and mind, encompassing more than most of us could bear, this dream "of what the living might become."

This was the dream that haunted, besieged, exalted him, that would not let him go. He dreamed a world where all were free to serve their sisters and brothers in compassion and hope, where fear had no dominion, where the resources of the nation were redistributed to meet the needs of the overwhelming majority of its people, where no one had to fear old age, or sickness, or being left alone.

Oh yes, he saw the rest, the other. Couldn't you tell it in his eyes? Didn't we feel the pain of what he saw, this brother from another planet? At all the funerals of his adopted children, sisters, brothers, mommas, and daddys, in all the jails, at every confrontation with dogs and guns and frightened, narrow, brutal men, he had seen us humans, plumbed the depths of our terror, our cruelty, and our fear, he had seen our selfishness and our blind ambition. But he never stopped looking there.

Always the dream pressed him on, inward, outward, deeper. In the depths of our eyes, roaming even then beyond the walls, he had found the fugitive hope, crouching in corners; he had seen the compassion, gnarled and unused, felt the love, unnamed, unrecognized, unclaimed; he had grasped the oneness, denied and bombed to shreds.

Something in this man saw the sister, brother, momma, fearful child in all the strangest places, faces, and he sang to us of what we might become, beyond walls. He sang in the night, sang the old Negro songs, sang the strong black songs, sang the African-sun-soaked songs, and beckoned us, red, white, brown, black, toward ourselves, told us, like Langston—dear brother Langston Hughes —told us, "America is a dream." And we of every hue and cry, we are the dreamers, creating, dreaming with him, singing with him, dancing with him, to Native American songs, Mexican songs, Scotch-Irish songs, German songs, African songs, Jewish songs, Vietnamese songs, Puerto Rican songs, Appalachian songs.

Organizing, marching, singing the songs, standing unflinching before the blows, going to jail, challenging all the killers of the dreams, he called us to sing, dream, and sing and build—and stand our ground, creating a new reality, a new nation, a new world, ready for the hero. He saw us dancing before we knew we could move. He recognized what we had not seen and was ready to live and die for it, for us.

Early in his movement toward us, back in the 1950s, he was sensing what he saw, saying, "I still believe that standing up for the truth of God is the greatest thing in the world . . . come what may." And for those of us who are getting ready, what truth of God could be greater than the truth of our rich, unexplored human possibilities, our fundamental oneness, our essential union with all life, and our responsibility to live out that truth, politically, economically, socially, spiritually, ecologically, cultur-ally—come what may—against all the systems of separation, dehumanization, and exploitation which deny "what the living may become"?

Are we ready to be what we may become? Oh nation of greatness, do we know who we are, really are, getting ready for our hero, and ourselves?

Long before the bullet struck, Martin was getting ready, mov-ing toward our rendezvous. In the little book of poetry, John Dixon caught a glimpse of the hero becoming, and shared his insight with us:

In an age when courage is measured by destruction, his courage was the courage of love. In an age when men are commodities with a price, he believed in the reality of persons. In an age afraid to believe, his faith was as innocent as a child's. In an age when subtlety of intelligence serves profit or power, his mind sought the liberations of peace.

What embarrassing words: courage, faith, love, liberation, peace. Haven't they been outlawed yet? Lock doors, put troops at the gate, guard the legislative halls against courage and faith, against liberation, love, and peace! But here comes the dead man, living, walking, still becoming. He comes piercing our walls, planting courage, planting faith, planting love and peace toward the center of our hearts, reminding us that "intelligence" was not meant to be another word for espionage, spying, and dirty tricks, that doctorates do not have to be sold to the highest bidders, that there is another way, a liberating way, to be shared, as he used to say "by no D's and PhD's." Are we ready? Is this implacable lover really our hero? Hero of a nation not yet born, but borning? God, are those the pangs we feel?

The poet continues:

He was never perfect in wisdom nor ever pretended to be. He was never perfect in conduct, nor free from temptations nor ever pretended to be. But holiness is not perfection; it is transparency to the grace of God. This great, good man has shattered the pride, the selfishness of millions of men and women. If we now have the courage to begin anew, to remake what his life exposed, then he will be one of those chosen of God to be an instrument of grace.

My flawed and wounded brother-hero, who knew grace better than you? Battered, tossed, and sometimes possessed by your own powerful weaknesses, how did you go on, how did you stand, how did you begin again and again your struggle toward getting ready?

The poet says grace, amazing grace—how sweet, so sweet the sound—lost/found brother-hero, the poet says grace. Depending on it, immersed in it, forever opened to it, by it, you now walk through our walls of guilt and fear and take our battered hands and broken lives and hold us, gently strong, as we rise, again, and again. For we, like you, are chosen to choose, to become what we might be—means of grace, sacraments of life for each other, rainbow warriors, peacemaking defenders of the earth, creators of a new world. Is that you, Brother Martin, singing, shouting:

> "Rise, shine, give God glory!"
> Getting ready for the hero,
> Rise, shine, our light is come.

Are you getting ready, Charlotte Nuby, you and your children? Who are you? Where are you now? The note in the book of poetry says only, "Charlotte Nuby was a ninth grade student at Haynes Junior High School, Nashville, Tennessee, when she wrote her poem on King's dream."

Growing up around Freedom Rides, sit-ins, wade-ins, kneel-ins, watching marchers wind through Nashville's streets, singing freedom songs in reverberating churches, hearing folks testify about jail and dogs and hoses and billy clubs and Jesus and grace and beloved community beyond race, you must have known something. Coming of age near Jim Lawson and Diane Nash, near Jim Bevel and Jim Zwerg, listening to Kelly Miller Smith and John Lewis and all the hosts of Nashville's valiant, crucial army of freedom fighters, your child heart had its own understanding of liberation heroes. So when the word from Memphis erupted within us all, you were already becoming woman, writing:

> There was a man who loved this land.
> But hated discrimination
> And took his stand. . . .
> He was shunned and criticized by some;
> But he always said
> "We shall Overcome."
> He fought for all to see the light

And in their hearts they knew he was
    right.
He fought for equality; he fought for peace
And knew that someday
All prejudice would cease.
He fought against war; he fought against
    strife
Until a sniper's bullet took his life.
And when we say our prayers of silence
Remember he died for non-violence.

Some things are very clear in the ninth grade, aren't they, Charlotte? Our hero loved us, loved this land, kept seeing beyond our walls, kept tugging at our consciences and our hearts, kept urging us toward what we might become. And took his stand, yes, sometimes against the gates of hell, took his stand. Fought hard, didn't he, Charlotte, fought hard for those he loved. Fought against our mistreatment of black folks, napalmed folks, missile-targeted folks. Took his stand, Charlotte.

Tell it to your children. (Do you have some? What are their names?) Tell it to your nieces and nephews, tell it to your Sunday school children, tell it to your public school children, tell it to your Afrikan Free School children, tell it to your many-mani-cured-acres-private-school children, tell it to your welfare children, Charlotte.

This was no "nice Christian minister," only; no "great orator," primarily; no "civil rights leader," alone; this was more than a dreamer of black and white children holding hands. Tell them, Sister Charlotte, wherever you are, that he fought for the poor, that he fought against greed, that he was against war, that he was ready to give his life for the way of nonviolence in the struggle for truth and justice.

When you were in the seventh grade, my young sister, and Brother Martin was hemmed up against the wall by all the under-standable fires of rage exploding in black communities across the nation, he declared again and again, "I still believe in nonviolence, and no one is going to turn me around on that. If every Negro in the United States turns to violence, I am going to stand up and be the only voice to say that it is wrong."

When he said it, Charlotte, he made it clear that he meant it for Vietnam as well as Chicago, for poor people and for generals. Then he spent the rest of his life, a brief life, trying to fashion creative, audacious models of nonviolent resistance, trying to transform the values and structures of this nation toward compassionate, radical commitment to the poor, toward a new vision of democratic participation and decision making for us all, moving toward what we might become.

Remind the children that this man with a doctorate died in the midst of a struggle for garbage workers. Tell them, Charlotte, that he was calling black and white young people to refuse to serve in a U.S. military force that is so readily used to suppress poor people and their revolutions. Let them hear Brother Martin calling for another service, a more constructive, creative way of standing up for this land that he loved.

When you say your silent prayers, Charlotte, pray for the children—yours, mine, all—for the courage, the wisdom, and the strength they need to take their heroic stand in the midst of a land that romanticizes violence everywhere. When you enter the silence, dear sister, pray for us older ones—you, me, all—that we may remember who our hero really was, and how he loved us, and what he was calling us to do, to be, to become. Find someone, Charlotte, wherever you are, and hold hands with them, and work with them, and take your stand together.

It's easier when you're holding hands, Charlotte. Martin, though often surrounded by crowds, too often walked alone, with no covenanted community of sharing, seeking, bonded folks. Find what he didn't have, daughter. Get ready. Take your stand, Charlotte Nuby, wherever you've gone from Haynes Junior High. Take your stand. There's a hero waiting. Teach the children. There's a new nation to be born. Getting ready.

To teach the children is to get ready. To rescue them from the slick appeals of militarism, materialism, hedonism, and social irresponsibility is to get ready. For without such nurturing care we allow the poet N. Ellsworth Bunce no space for his vision:

> Where one dies thousands rise
> For Martyrs are made to
>   multiply
>   The stars catch the sound
>   The wind carries the word. . . .
> In the silence
> Where he once stood
> The children grow
> The poor gather
> And those now mourning know
> They shall be comforted
> —Comforted—and fulfilled.

Poets and sweepers, mothers and teachers, deacons and barbers, cashiers and fathers, pastors and nurses, teach the children, everyone, for they are the thousands (and we are the thousands) who must rise to meet the hero. They are the catchers of the falling stars, the riders on the rising wind. Teach the children, let them grow, knowing the hero as a strong man, hearing his voice, seeing his face as lover of this nation, as implacable foe of injustice and exploitation, as courageous speaker of the truth to senators and streetboys, as dreamer of a land where the weak, the sick, the old, the poor, and the tender young become the center of our attention, the focus of our "defense," the apple of our eye.

Gather with others to teach the children, by word and by deed. Conspire, band together in communities of resistance, healing, and hope. Wean them and us from the terrible thought that they become men—or women—by becoming uniformed killers of people and dreams. There is a better way. The brother hero was on pilgrimage toward that way, searching for that way, creating that way. He was obsessed by a voice that would not let him go, drawing him, pressing him on the way, saying, "Blessed are the peacemakers. . . ."

Is it too late to teach the children? Can the churches, with whom he carried on so fierce a lover's quarrel, still get ready, committing themselves to explore alternative ways for the children to become women and men by working with the poor, gathering with the Native Americans in their struggles for survival and renewal, building armies of heroes in the inner cities, developing new links of compassionate solidarity overseas?

Is it too late for us, any, all, to walk through the Official Hero walls around King and enter into the last years of his life, dance imaginatively into his dream process, open beyond it to the dreams of saints and lovers over generations of struggle and create new realities, take our stand, teaching the children, with and without words, that there is another way, a better way than the way of weapons and war, to be all they can be?

Too late to get ready? Can't be. Late, but not too late, for we are here in this now, and it is ours. And the poor are gathering, and there is much mourning, and the thousands and the tens of thousands (are the faces familiar, hero faces, our faces?) are being called to comfort and fulfill.

On April 6, 1968, two days after the bullet of fear and greed, of racism and militarism, and of ignorance and blindness had finally caught up with her husband, Coretta Scott King offered her own prose poem to the world:

> He knew that at any moment his physical life could be cut short, and we faced this possibility squarely and honestly . . . without bitterness or hatred. . . . He gave his life for the poor of the world—the garbage workers of Memphis and the peasants of Vietnam. Nothing hurt him more than that humankind could find no way to solve problems except through violence. He gave his life in search of a more excellent way, a creative rather than a destructive way. We intend

to go on in search of that way, and I hope that you who loved and admired him would join us in fulfilling his dream.

The invitation remains. Clear, precise, direct: Fulfill the dream, fulfill the dreamer, fulfill the people, fulfill the nation. Bring it into actuality. Let it be born. Let us be born.

Calling all friends, lovers, and admirers. The invitation is here, still here. R.S.V.P. Now. It's getting late, and Charlotte is waiting with her children, to stand and walk and struggle and fly with all who will go with the hero, continuing the search, life-long search, soul-deep struggle, for the "more excellent way."

R.S.V.P. Get ready, if you please.

Returning to the source, the last half of Gwendolyn Brooks's poem closes the small book and opens the great path:

> His Dream still wishes to anoint
>   the barricades of faith and of control.
> His word still burns the center of the sun,
>   above the thousands and the
>   hundred thousands.
> The word was Justice. It was spoken.
> So it shall be spoken.
> So it shall be done.

Getting ready. The balm in Gilead flows, and we are anointed, sanctified, rescued from the mainstream, delivered to the ancient river. And the dream expands, explodes around, within, like a burning, rising sun filling every crevice of our trembling, yearning hearts. Justice. Compassion. Peace, Liberation. Love. Let them be spoken, let them be done, in us, in me. Getting ready.

Martin, Fannie Lou, Dorothy, Amzie, Bapu, A.J., Mickey, Sojourner, Clarence—all of you, we're getting ready. Charlotte's getting ready. The children are getting ready, to catch stars, to ride winds, to do the word, to fulfill the dream. Don't know about the nation, Martin, but some justice-loving, people-serving, peace-making folks of every color and condition are getting ready. I see them, feel them, carry them in my bones. Rainbow warriors, anointed, burning bright, getting ready.

Walk through our walls. It's an invitation. R.S.V.P. Soon. 'Cause it's late, and we've found ourselves: We, too, are the heroes, singing, dancing, unrelenting heroes. And ain't no grave can hold our body down. Are you ready?

CHAPTER 3

MARTIN KING, BURNING BUSHES, AND US

Revisiting the March on Washington

(Written for the twentieth anniversary of the 1963 March on Washington.)

We are marching on Washington—again. Buses with banners flapping in the wind are coming from every direction. Cars filled with tired but hopeful pilgrims are on the road. Train stations and airports will soon be alive with vision-seekers—again.

Churches are getting ready. Members are making sandwiches, mopping basement floors, putting up cots, laying out sleeping bags, praying again in all the ways people pray for special times and places. Soon we will be singing again, grasping hands, swaying, brushing away tears, holding reunions, sharing precious memories—again.

And what does it all mean? Why are we marching for "jobs, peace, and freedom" twenty years after that first powerful event on the Mall? The question is not rhetorical. It has been asked many times along the way to Washington. It is a necessary question, good for all souls. Why are we gathering again in the same place, in the same way, with apparently the same goals, with many (but not all, no, not all) of the same people?

For some of us, it's a matter of remembering, commemorating, honoring the past, calling attention to how it was when black people and their white allies led a movement for freedom, justice, and new humanity (much, much more, much, much deeper than something called "civil rights") that began to shake the foundations of this nation and offered hope, models, and music to hundreds of millions of humans around the world.

It is, of course, understandable that some of us see the event as a time to try to recapture the great electric energy that was created in our lives and in this country by "the Movement," as we called it, an energy that was focused in a peculiar manner in the complex, courageous person and unparalleled rhetorical power of Martin Luther King, Jr. Some of us are coming to Washington again because we need in some way to see him, feel him, hear him again. Somehow we need to remember the fallen brother who was both a marvelous creation and creator of the most powerful continuing social force for freedom that the nation has ever known. We feel a need to lift him up, and in doing so to elevate and celebrate the lives, the hopes, the deaths—and rebirths—of all the anonymous millions he represented.

For others, especially younger others, the marching may be a way to join history, to participate even for a few hours in what we felt we missed, what we want to claim as our own. For a day, perhaps, one hot August day in D.C., in 1983, it may be like a pilgrimage to a hallowed ground. Standing there, walking there, we may feel that we are surrounded, enveloped by burning bushes, each manifesting a powerful, divine presence. That will be all right, for such holy, historical ground is ours to claim. It was developed for us by thousands, tens of thousands, hundreds of thousands of women, men, and children like us, in every generation, who were laying the foundations with their living and dying, creating the sacred space with their courageous commitment and undying love; men, women and children who finally broke loose in the late 1950s and took many names—like Rosa Parks and E.D. Dixon, like Fanny Lou Hamer and Slater King, like Medgar Evers, Ruby Doris Smith, Ralph Featherstone, and William Moore, like Anne Braden and Herbert Lee, Bob Moses and Diane Nash Bevel, who took on the names of Malcolm X, Annelle Ponder, and Elizabeth Eckford, who became John Lewis and Bill Hanson,

In March 1965 King attends a memorial Mass for slain civil rights worker Mrs. Viola Liuzzo.

Moma Dolly and Charlie Cobb, who were called Ella Baker, Charles Sherrod, Septima Clarke, and many thousands more.

But mostly the names were our names, representing our lives, and through accident, inscrutable circumstances, media maneuvering, and the movement of spiritual vectors beyond our comprehension, Martin King became their voice, our voice. On that August day in 1963 he proclaimed his dream, our dream, to a listening, yearning world, to our own listening, yearning, unquiet hearts.

Because something connected to that time continues to move deeply within us, we are compelled to return, in person, in spirit, moving toward Washington, prepared to march again, perhaps hoping for some magic in these desperate times. But there is danger in the return of these natives, in our attempt to touch our spiritual home, our Movement base again. And that danger must be named, must be faced, must be transcended if we are to move toward the maturity that is yet in store for us, if we are to continue to create new, humane realities for our children, for all children, in this land, beyond these shores.

Perhaps at the center of the danger is the paradox: in the very act of claiming our history we may deny it. In the moment of remembering we may be tempted to forget.

What do I mean? I mean that the history of our struggle for the transformation of ourselves and this country, and the story of King's dream neither began nor ended in 1963. That seems simple, but is not always easy to remember. For the soft, sentimental, nostalgic parts of each of us would like to bask in the sun of that vaguely remembered summer's day (forgetting the blood that was shed the same year in Danville, Virginia, Birmingham, Alabama, Jackson, Mississippi, and a hundred lesser-known, unnamed places, to provide the creation power for the march). We would like to forget the conflicts in vision, strategy, and principles that erupted right on the speaker's platform that day, and instead carefully bathe ourselves in the euphoria of King's "Free at Last," peroration, as if it were meant to be a final statement rather than a rallying call to the next demanding stages of our struggle.

We would like to forget that Martin Luther King, Jr., did not ascend into the skies from the Lincoln Memorial in 1963, but spent five hard, searching, experimenting, stumbling, sometimes lonely, and often beleaguered years trying to find the way toward a humanized America, jamming so much change, growth, and groping into those years that it could be said of him as it was first said of Malcolm X, "He became much more than there was time for him to be." We would like to forget that it was not the weaver of gentle, sunny dreams of freedom who was shot down on a balcony in Memphis, Tennessee. Rather it was a man who was recently described by a careful scholar in this way: "In the last twelve months of his life, King represented a far greater political threat to the reigning American government than he ever had before."

It is that courageous brother who calls us now to move beyond nostalgia, beyond collective amnesia, beyond mere repetition, and to remember our tasks, his tasks, the work to which he set himself as he rapidly outgrew the limitations of August, 1963. If we consider him for a while, if we focus on the three goals of the earlier march that now repeat themselves among us—"Jobs, Peace, and Freedom"—it is not hard to see that there was a long road toward maturity for King and the Movement beyond the march in 1963. If we look closely and listen well, we will probably see, too, that there is a long, magnificent and harrowing way that we shall have to go beyond Washington in 1983. It is a road that we can take with Martin and many others from that time (we focus on him now only for the sake of economy and clarity); it is a road that will also move us beyond him toward the wilderness, to the uncharted ways, to the discoveries and inventions that we must boldly create in the quest for a new society.

But let us go back to Martin. (Or will most of us have to go *forward* from where we are now to catch up with where he was when he left us?) By the time he was cut down in the line of love and duty, he had looked hard at the dream, seriously pondered what was required of him, of us, of this nation, of this world to move with integrity toward jobs, peace, and freedom. By 1968 Martin knew there could be no adequate jobs for black people in the United States until the nation had turned itself toward the unconditional goal of providing fulfilling work and adequate income for everyone in the society. By then, King also knew that such a nonutopian goal could not be achieved here unless the fundamental economic, political, and value structures of the U.S.A. were challenged and transformed. There was no doubt in his mind that our current American capitalism, built on the struggle for economic, military, and cultural hegemony in the world, could not provide the spirit, the motivation, or the structures to make work available to all persons who were capable of working.

At the same time, King was slowly turning away from the New Deal-inspired dream that the federal government (locked as it was into a deadly alliance with an almost autonomous military and with the U.S.A.-based transnational corporate structures) had any, or desired any, compassionate solutions—regardless of the color, gender, or political leanings of the president, regardless of which of our major parties was "in power." For by the end of his life he had realized that the black freedom movement was, in his words, "exposing the evils that are deeply rooted in the whole structure of our society. It reveals systemic rather than superficial flaws and suggests that radical reconstruction of society itself is the real issue to be faced."

At the same time, it is important to note that Martin was not inclined to jump to the conclusion that any socialism that we have seen anywhere offered an alternate model for the "reconstruction" of this, the most technologically advanced society in the world. For him, the answers, the models, the hopes, the new constructions were still in the hearts and minds of all those men and women who were being drawn away from the old and working their lives toward a new way. As he groped toward answers, models, directions that are not yet manifest, as he tried to inspire others toward the radical path, King knew instinctively, and said it more and more clearly, that we would be unfaithful to our own best history of struggle and to the hopes of the exploited peoples of the world, if black folk in the U.S.A. were to settle for what is now called "a fair share" (and what was known in the sixties as "a piece of the pie")—some proportionate cut of the wealth amassed by this nation's military-industrial empire. For he understood how fundamentally the structures of military and economic domination are built on the exploitation and deprivation of our own poor people (for instance, "structural unemployment" is immorally accepted as necessary to our questionable prosperity), and depends on the exploitation and manipulation of the poor peoples of the raw-materials-producing nations of the world. In other words, he knew by definition, that the shares of *this* system could never be fair.

(How would history have judged us if our black foreparents had somehow managed to accompany the marauding American armies into Mexico in the 1840s and asked for our "fair share" of the stolen, conquered land? And what would our children now be saying if in any large numbers we had followed the U.S. troops on their genocidal sweep across the plains, stained with the blood of the Natives of the land, asking for our "fair share" of their sacred places?)

That is why King's cry from the heart for peace became louder and louder as the U.S. escalated its brutal war against the Vietnamese people and their hopes for self-determination. For not only did he see his nation robbing essential resources and energies from the great human needs of our own burning cities, but the leaders of our country were manipulating the poor young men and their families, often refusing to develop civilian jobs for them, instead sending them on errands of fire, brutality, and death against other poor, nonwhite people thousands of miles away. (Remember the words of Muhammad Ali as he refused to go: "No Vietcong ever called me Nigger!")

Following this path, it was not surprising then that by 1967–68 Martin was telling us all that the peace we needed was one that stretched far beyond the end of particular wars, even so horrible a war as the one in Vietnam. For him, Americans could pursue effective peace only as we recognized how intrinsically it is joined to justice, especially justice in the uses and distribution of the world's common resources. Indeed, Martin repeatedly said the United States was "on the wrong side of a world revolution," one in which the poor and landless people are determined to press relentlessly toward justice, toward land, toward self-development and self-determination, toward their own best humanity. As Martin saw it, the political and economic leaders of our nation had positioned themselves on the side of the small minority of the powerful, resource-dominating, reactionary "leaders" of the Third World nations, men and women who are determined to contain and control the poor of their own nations, for a variety of ideological, economic, racial, and personal reasons. Martin saw our own government and corporate forces using the smoke screen of "anticommunism" to win over our people to this fundamentally antirevolutionary role.

Constantly probing toward the roots of the problems, King said that it was only as we changed our values and our basic international allegiances, only as we were willing to change our lifestyles and back off from our inordinate and inequitable demands on the world's finite resources—only then, he said, could we begin to play our role as peacemakers. Only as we are willing as citizens and humans to deal with the "triple threat" of materialism, militarism, and racism, he said, only as we abandoned our misinformed and manipulated anticommunism, only then could we begin a true march for peace (and jobs and freedom, and democracy—and humanity), a true movement toward the poor nations of the world. Without such a turning, Martin claimed, this nation's people of good will and concern would be protesting our military's involvement in new Vietnams all over the world, wherever the poor were shut off, beginning, he said, with Latin America.

Lest anyone think that his call for change was directed only toward white people, all we need to do is look around us, look within us, and see how much over the past fifteen to twenty years we black folks have decided (consciously or not) to fight racism by seeking for "equal opportunity" or a "fair share" in the nation's militarism and its materialism. In other words, we have chosen to struggle against one of the "triple threats" by joining the other two, a destructive choice.

Whether or not Martin was talking to black people *then,* he is surely talking to us now, and it is in our best interest to listen. For in our successful challenges to official segregation, in our movement through the partly open doors, we have imbibed much of the spirit that our brother identified as the spirit of greed, belligerency, fearful callousness, and individualism, a spirit that makes us anti-poor people, anti-immigrants, that creates injustice, that makes for war. Ask not to whom the King speaks. He is our brother, our King, and he speaks to us.

If we listen to him in the last years of his life, we hear Martin desperately calling us away from the mentality which seeks a piece of the American pie, which makes for American wars. Rather, he urged upon himself, on each of us, on all of us, a revolution in our values. He challenged us to search for a new recipe, create a new vision of what needs to be baked, develop a new pie based on compassion and human solidarity rather than on maximum profits.

He called us away from our spiritually debilitating worship of material wealth. Looking to the poor on every hand, understanding something of the relationship between poverty and exploitation at home and abroad, refusing to be silenced by the allurements of middle-class comforts, by the governmentally orchestrated threats of personal blackmail or the repeated threats of violent death, King continued his search for audacious solutions. For instance, in his last months he proposed that those persons who wanted peace, who believed that peace demanded nonviolent revolutionary change in the U.S.A. should form an alliance without regard to national borders with the men and women who wanted to experiment with this unconventional means of working for peace and justice in Latin America and elsewhere. Of course, he knew that anyone who worked for justice in Latin America, anyone who sought land for the poor, anyone who moved toward local people's control over their raw materials would have to challenge and oppose the political, military, and economic status quo leadership of the United States

—and their powerful counterparts in other sectors of the so-called developed world.

In other words, Martin saw no easy peace, no cheap grace. By the time of his death, peace for him was tied to new value systems, new ways of defining our personal and national needs, new disciplines of creative mass-based, nonviolent movement. By the time the garbage workers called him to Memphis, he saw their struggle as part of the work of peace. For peace was linked to economic justice and to the radical redistribution of wealth, nationally and internationally. His concern for the poor had burst the boundaries of race and nationality, had transformed the meaning of the Movement he had helped to create, had allowed him to grope toward creative responses to the history raging all around him. And as he moved toward the wilderness, into the unknown and uncertain, as he tried to transform himself, his organization, and supporters, moving constantly toward the Promised Land of faith and courage, seeking to find ways to create that which did not yet exist, he was constantly calling us, black us, white us, Chicano us, Native American us, Asian American us, all of us.

His call was an urgent invitation to turn sharply away from our commitment to an ever-ascending, ever-stifling, "higher standard of living," and to set our faces in compassion toward the poor of every color of every land. He was calling us to give our imaginations, our skills, our training, our energies, and perhaps our lives to the tasks of eliminating the great human scourges of hunger, exploitation, and war, to find in such work the roots of peace, the roots of our humanity, the presence of God.

One of the last times I saw him alive, he was meeting in Atlanta in the winter of 1968 with a group of Native Americans, Chicanos, Appalachian whites, and urban black people—in addition to representatives of his basic Southern black constituency and his national church allies. He was looking for a way to draw all these folks together in the struggle for a new peace with justice, for a new citizenship based on responsibility and hope, for a new American nation. The room was palpably charged with the tension of uncertainty and the hope of great, though guarded, expectations. That was meant to be the vision and the spirit which informed the deepest levels of the Poor People's Campaign of 1968. It was to be the joining of all the causes, all the people. "He became much more than there was time for him to be."

And what was his vision of freedom by then? It was inseparable from his visions of adequate work and peace, and it was in the process of becoming, constantly improvised, responding to the demands of urban rebellions, Black Power explosions, thousands of body bags returning from Vietnam, challenges to his leadership from every side. Still he moved forward, working out his sense of freedom, developing it as he moved from Oslo to Mississippi to Chicago to Washington to Memphis and hundreds of other places along the way—and through many dark, restless nights when sleep would not come. He worked it out.

By 1968 he had not forsaken his essential March on Washington definition of freedom as the power of children and adults to link hands and lives across racial lines, but he was expanding, transcending, constantly relating it to his own sense of vocation. So when men and women, black and white, asked him in 1967–68 why he had turned so much of his attention to the war in Vietnam, to the call for peace through international justice, when they accused him of deserting *their* image of a black freedom movement, he challenged them to expand their understanding of his work and theirs. He urged on them, on us, a greater, richer vision of freedom.

Responding to their questions, he testified concerning some of the deepest sources of his own freedom, revealed the continuing process toward the unifying of his concerns. One base for that unification, one basis for the freedom he sensed was his commitment to the ministry of the gospel of Jesus Christ. In 1967, King said, "To me, the relationship of this ministry to the making of peace is so obvious that I sometimes marvel at those who ask me why I am speaking against the war. . . . Have they forgotten that my ministry is in obedience to the One who loved his enemies so fully that he died for them?" Here peace and freedom were joined. Here was a freedom that opened him to move beyond the bound-

aries of race, nationality, and idealogy, to reach out to the
suffering wherever they might be, even those, especially those who
were dying under the searing napalm and fragmentation bombs
and heavy lies of his own country's military forces. (In that vein he
began to demand that the churches—black and white—press on
beyond pious statements regarding Christian love and actively
demonstrate the radical freedom of that love by teaching their
young people what Jesus said about loving enemies, by opening
them to the option of conscientious objection to military service,
as a way toward conscientious commitment to unconditional
love—the ultimate source of freedom.)

In addition, Martin closed his life while loudly proclaiming his
fundamental identity as a child of God, saying that he was thereby
related by ties deeper than human blood or government rulings,
or creedal formulations, to all the people of the world. This was a
magnificent freedom, releasing him to see himself, to see God, to
see humanity in a new light, and then to act in new ways. He
called black people and all who wanted to join the march toward
a new freedom to envision themselves not simply moving away
from slavery and oppression, away from racism and discrimina-
tion, away from exploitation and domination. Rather (like Frantz
Fanon in the last pages of *The Wretched of the Earth*) King urged us
to see ourselves moving forward always, urgently holding
ourselves in the vanguard of humanity's best possibilities. He
asked us to see our freedom as empowering us to create new
values, to envision a new society. He challenged us to mold our
freedom as a power to break beyond self-centered goals, to work
for a new humanity. That was what he meant when, toward the
end of one of the last, full, published expressions of his own
movement he said, "Let us rededicate ourselves to the long and
bitter—but beautiful—struggle for a new world. This is the
calling of the children of God." Nothing less is worthy of us, King
said. Nothing less is worthy of the creator God.

By the end of his life, in 1968, Martin King had moved decades
beyond the March on Washington of 1963. So, in 1983, as we
tread our way back to that hallowed ground for a moment, a day,

of commemoration and nostalgia, let us remember that he is no longer there. He has moved on ahead of us. By 1968 he was already ahead of where most of us dare to be now. But if we are to be faithful to him and to the tens of thousands who created him, if we are to be faithful to our children and our own best selves, faithful to the blood, then we must move on, we must press beyond this powerful, temporary, historical ritual.

It is urgent that we move on. There are new grounds to be hallowed, new bushes to set afire with the truth of divine compassion, with the creative, sacramental power of free women and men. We must move forward to keep up, to find the King who has continued to move, to grow far beyond 1963, beyond 1968, beyond 1983.

We honor him best now by moving audaciously, gratefully beyond him. No search for jobs, peace, and freedom can develop in integrity unless it comes to terms with the vision of Martin King in 1967–68 and then presses courageously beyond. Anything less would be a hoax, a betrayal of our ancestors and our children, a denial of the dream, a longing to return to the fleshpots of our one-time captors. We are capable of much more than that. We were meant to be free. Nothing less is worthy of us.

We have not come, have not been led, this far to turn back. We go forward or die. Do you see the burning bushes ahead?

CHAPTER 4

BEYOND AMNESIA

Martin Luther King, Jr.,
and the Future of America

In the 1970s a fascinating variety of voices began to press the nation to decide where it stood concerning the memory and meaning of Martin Luther King, Jr. As we instinctively sought an easy way to deal with the unrelenting power of this disturber of all unjust peace, it became increasingly clear that most of those who were leading the campaign for the establishment of a national holiday had chosen, consciously or unconsciously, to allow King to become a "convenient hero," to try to tailor him to the shape and mood of mainstream, liberal/moderate America.

Symbolic of the direction taken by the campaign has been the unremitting focus on the 1963 March on Washington, the never-ending repetition of the great speech and its dream metaphor, the sometimes innocent and sometimes manipulative boxing of King into the relatively safe categories of "civil rights leader," "great orator," harmless dreamer of black and white children on the hillside. And surely nothing could be more ironic or amnesiac than having Vice-President George Bush, the former head of the Central Intelligence Agency, the probable White House overseer of Contra actions, speaking official words in King's honor. Or was it more ironic to watch the representatives of the Marine Corps, carrying fresh memories from the invasion of Grenada and from their training for Libya and for Nicaragua, playing "We Shall Overcome," while the bust of the prince of nonviolence was

King denounces slum conditions in Chicago, February 1966.

placed in the Capitol rotunda, without a word being spoken about his soul-deep commitment to the ways of peace?

It appears as if the price for the first national holiday honoring a black man is the development of a massive case of national amnesia concerning who that black man really was. At both personal and collective levels, of course, it is often the case that amnesia is not ultimately harmful to the patient. However, in this case it is very dangerous, for the things we have chosen to forget about King (and about ourselves) constitute some of the most hopeful possibilities and resources for our magnificent and very needy nation. Indeed, I would suggest that we Americans have chosen amnesia rather than continue King's painful, uncharted, and often disruptive struggle toward a more perfect union. I would also suggest that those of us who are historians and citizens have a special responsibility to challenge the loss of memory, in ourselves and others, to allow our skills in probing the past to become resources for healing and for hope. In other words, if Martin King cannot challenge those who would make him a harmless black icon, then *we* surely can raise such a challenge—assuming that we are still alive.

Although there are many points at which our challenge to the comfortable images might be put forth, I believe that the central encounters with King that begin to take us beyond the static March-on-Washington, "integrationist," "civil rights leader" image are located in Chicago and Mississippi in 1966. During the winter of that year King moved north. He was driven by the fires of Watts and the early hot summers of 1964 and 1965. Challenged and nurtured by the powerful commitment of Malcolm X to the black street forces, he was also compelled by his own deep compassion for the urban black community—whose peculiar problems were not fundamentally addressed by the essential civil rights laws so dearly won in the South. Under such urgent compulsion, King left his familiar southern base and stepped out on very unfamiliar turf. For Hamlin Avenue on Chicago's blighted West Side was a long way from the marvelous, dramatic, and costly victories of Selma, St. Augustine, and Birmingham; and Mayor Richard Daley was a consummate professional compared to the sheriffs, mayors, and police commissioners of the South. But King had made his choice, and it is one that we dare not forget.

By 1966 King had made an essentially religious commitment to the poor, and he was prepared to say:

> I choose to identify with the underprivileged. I choose to identify with the poor. I choose to give my life for the hungry. I choose to give my life for those who have been left out of the sunlight of opportunity. I choose to live for and with those who find themselves seeing life as a long and desolate corridor with no exit sign. This is the way I'm going. If it means suffering a little bit, I'm going that way. If it means sacrificing, I'm going that way. If it means dying for them, I'm going that way, because I heard a voice saying, "Do something for others."[1]

We understood nothing about the King whose life ended in the midst of a struggle for garbage workers if we miss that earlier offering of himself to the struggle against poverty in America, to the continuing battle for the empowerment of the powerless—in this nation, in Vietnam, in South Africa, in Central America, and beyond.

In a sense, it was that commitment that led him back south from Chicago to Mississippi in the late spring of 1966, as he responded to the attempted assassination of James Meredith, taking up with others that enigmatic hero's "march against fear." There on the highways of the Magnolia State we have a second crucial encounter with the forgotten King. He was an embattled leader, the King who was challenged, chastened, and inspired by the courageous, often foolhardy Young Turks of the Student Nonviolent Coordinating Committee. He was attentive to those veterans of the struggle who raised the cry for "Black Power," who made public the long simmering challenge to King's leadership, who increasingly voiced their doubts about the primacy of nonviolence as a way of struggle, and who seemed prepared at that juncture to read whites out of the Movement. One of the most important aspects of the Meredith March for King's development was the question the young people raised in many forms: "Dr. King, why do you want us to love white folks before we even love ourselves?" From then on the issues of black self-love, of black and white power, and of the need to develop a more militant form of nonviolence that could challenge and enlist the rising rage of urban black youth were never far from King's consciousness. Along with his deepening commitment to the poor, those were the subjects and questions that did much to shape the last years of the hero we have forgotten.

One of the reasons for our amnesia, of course, is the fact that the forgotten King is not easy to handle now. Indeed, he never was. In 1967, after spending two hectic weeks traveling with the impassioned black prophet, David Halberstam, a perceptive journalist, reported that

> King has decided to represent the ghettos, he will work in them and speak for them. But their voice is harsh and alienated. If King is to speak for them truly, then his voice must reflect theirs; it, too, must be alienated, and it is likely to be increasingly at odds with the rest of American society.[2]

Halberstam was right, but only partly so. After the Selma marches of 1965, King's voice did sound harsher in its criticism of the mainstream American way of life and its dominant values—including the assumption that the United States had the right to police the world for "free enterprise." Not only did the white mainstream object to such uncompromising social criticism from a "civil rights leader" who was supposed to know his place, but many respectable black people were increasingly uncomfortable as well.[3] For some of them were making use of the fragile doorways that the freedom movement had helped open. Others, after years of frustration, were finally being promoted into the positions of responsibility and higher earning that their skills and experience should have earlier made available. Too often, King was considered a threat to them as well, especially as his commitment to the poor drove him to increasingly radical assessments of the systemic flaws in the American economic order, an order they had finally begun to enjoy.

But Halberstam, a man of words, saw only part of the picture. King did more than *speak* for the ghettos. He was committed to mobilizing and organizing them for self-liberating action. That was his deeper threat to the status quo, beyond words, beyond alienation. That was what King's friend Rabbi Abraham Heschel surely understood when in early 1968 he introduced King to an assembly of rabbis in these words: "Martin Luther King, Jr., is a voice, a vision and a way. I call upon every Jew to harken to his voice, to share his vision, to follow in his way. The whole future of America will depend on the impact and influence of Dr. King."[4]

Part of what we have forgotten, then, is King's vision, beyond the appealing dream of black and white children holding hands, beyond the necessary goal of "civil rights." From the outset, he held a vision for all America, often seeing the black movement as much more than a quest for rights—identifying it as a struggle "to redeem the soul of America." By the end of his life, no one who paid attention could mistake the depth and meaning of that vision. At his last annual convention of the Southern Christian Leadership Conference (SCLC) in 1967, King announced, "We must go from this convention and say, 'America, you must be born again . . . your whole structure must be changed.'" He insisted that "the problem of racism, the problem of economic exploitation, and the problem of war are all tied together." These, King said, were "the triple evils" that the freedom movement must address as it set itself to the challenge of "restructuring the whole of American society." This was the vision behind the call he issued in his final public speech in Memphis on April 3, 1968: "Let us move on in these powerful days, these days of challenge to make America what it ought to be. We have an opportunity to make America a better nation."[5]

That final speech was delivered to a crowd of some two thousand persons, mostly black residents of Memphis who had come out in a soaking rain to hear King and to support the garbage workers' union in its struggle for justice. King's challenge to his last movement audience reminds us that he also carried a large and powerful vision concerning the role of black people and others of the "disinherited" in American society. His vision had always included more than "rights" or "equal opportunity." On December 5, 1955, at the public meeting that launched the Montgomery bus boycott—and Martin Luther King, Jr.—into the heart of twentieth-century history, King had announced,

> We, the disinherited of this land, we who have been op-pressed so long, are tired of going through the long night of captivity. And now we are reaching out for the daybreak of freedom and justice and equality.

As a result of that decision and that movement, King said,

> when the history books are written in the future somebody will have to say "There lived a race of people, of black people, fleecy locks and black complexion, a people who had the moral courage to stand up for their rights, and thereby they injected a new meaning into the veins of history and of civi-lization." And we're gonna do that. God grant that we will do it before it's too late.[6]

From the beginning to the end, the grand vision, the magnifi-cent obsession, the audacious hope for America and its disinher-ited, never left him. Only in the light of that dual vision can we understand his voice, especially in its increasing alienation from the mainstream, in its urgent movement beyond the black and white civil rights establishment. In his last years, the vision led him to call repeatedly for "a reconstruction of the entire society, a revo-lution of values."[7] Only as we recapture the wholeness of King's vision can we understand his conclusion in 1967 that "something is wrong with capitalism as it now stands in the United States." Only then can we grasp his word to his coworkers in SCLC: "We are not interested in being integrated into *this* value structure. Power must be relocated." The vision leads directly to the voice, calling for "a radical redistribution of economic and political power" as the only way to meet the real needs of the poor in America.[8]

When our memories allow us to absorb King's vision of a transformed America and a transforming force of black people and their allies, then we understand his powerful critique of the American war in Vietnam. After he struggled with his conscience about how open to make his opposition, after he endured intense pressure from Washington and from the civil rights establishment to be quiet, King's social vision and his religious faith stood him in good stead. He spoke out in a stirring series of statements and actions and declared:

> Never again will I be silent on an issue that is destroying the soul of our nation and destroying thousands and thousands of little children in Vietnam. . . . the time has come for a real prophecy, and I'm willing to go that road.[9]

Of course, King knew the costly way of prophets—as did the rabbi who called us "to follow in his way." We must assume that neither the black prophet nor his Jewish brother was speaking idle words, opening up frivolous ways. Rather those were visions, voices, and ways not meant to be forgotten.

Indeed, in a nation where the gap between rich and poor continues to expand with cruel regularity, where the numbers of black and Hispanic poor vie with each other for supremacy, where farmers and industrial workers are in profound crisis, where racism continues to proclaim its ruthless American presence, who can afford to forget King's compassionate and courageous movement toward justice? When the leaders of the country spew reams of lies to Congress and the people alike, in public and private statements, when the official keepers of the nation's best hopes seem locked in what King called "paranoid anticommunism," when we make cynical mercenaries out of jobless young people, sacrificing them to a rigid militarism that threatens the future of the world, do we dare repress the memory of a man who called us to struggle bravely toward "the daybreak of freedom and justice and equality"? Dare we forget a man who told us that "a nation that continues year after year to spend more money on military defense than on programs of social uplift is approaching spiritual death"?[10]

Clearly, we serve our scholarship and our citizenship most faithfully when we move ourselves and others beyond amnesia toward encounters with the jagged leading edges of King's prophetic vision. When we do that we recognize that Martin King himself was unclear about many aspects of the "way" he had chosen. In his commitment to the poor, in his search for the redistribution of wealth and power in America, in his relentless stand against war, in his determination to help America "repent of her modern economic imperialism," he set out on a largely uncharted way. Still, several polestars pointed the way for him, and they may suggest creative directions for our personal and collective lives.

As King searched for a way for Americans to press the nation toward its best possibilities, toward its next birth of freedom and justice, he held fast to several basic assumptions. Perhaps it will help to remember them:

1. He seemed convinced that in the last part of the twentieth century, anyone who still held a vision of "a more perfect union" and worked toward that goal had to be prepared to move toward fundamental, structural changes in the mainstream values, economic and political structures, and traditional leadership of American society.

2. King believed that those who are committed to a real, renewed war against poverty in America must recognize the connections between our domestic economic and political problems and the unhealthy position that we occupy in the military, economic, and political wards of the global community. In other words, what King called "the triple evils of racism, extreme materialism, and militarism" could be effectively fought only by addressing their reality and relationships in our life at home and abroad.[11]

3. Unlike many participants in current discussions of poverty and "the underclass" in American society, King assumed that his ultimate commitment was to help find the ways by which the full energies and angers of the poor could be challenged, organized, and engaged in a revolutionary process that confronted the status quo and opened creative new possibilities for them and for the nation. Surely this was what he meant when he said,

> the dispossessed of this nation—the poor, both white and Negro—live in a cruelly unjust society. They must organize a revolution against that injustice, not against the lives of . . . their fellow citizens, but against the structures through which the society is refusing . . . to lift the load of poverty.[12]

4. By the last months of his life, as King reflected on the developments in the freedom movement since its energies had turned northward and since some of its participants had begun to offer more radical challenges to the policies of the federal government at home and abroad, he reached an inescapable conclusion. The next stages of the struggle for a just American order could no longer expect even the reluctant support from the national government that the Southern-based movement had received since Montgomery. Now, he said, "We must formulate a program and we must fashion the new tactics which do not count on government good will, but instead serve to compel unwilling authorities to yield to the mandates of justice."[13]

5. Defying most of the conventional wisdom of black and white America, King determined to hold fast to both of his fundamental, religiously based commitments: to the humanizing empowerment and transformation of the poor and of the nation and to the way of nonviolence and creative peacemaking. His attempt to create a Poor People's Campaign to challenge—and, if necessary, to disrupt—the federal government on its home ground was an expression of this wild and beautiful experiment in creating nonviolent revolution. Planning for a massive campaign of civil disobedience carried on by poor people of all races, aided by their

un-poor allies, King announced, "We've got to make it known that until our problem is solved, America may have many, many days, but they will be full of trouble. There will be no rest, there will be no tranquility in this country until the nation comes to terms with [that problem]."[14]

For those who seek a gentle, nonabrasive hero whose recorded speeches can be used as inspirational resources for rocking our memories to sleep, Martin Luther King, Jr., is surely the wrong man. However, if there is even a chance that Rabbi Heschel was correct, that the untranquil King and his peace-disturbing vision, words, and deeds hold the key to the future of America, then another story unfolds, another search begins. We who are scholars and citizens then owe ourselves, our children, and our nation a far more serious exploration and comprehension of the man and the widespread movement with which he was identified.

Recently, the Afro-American liberation theologian Cornel West said of King, "As a proponent of nonviolent resistance, he holds out the only slim hope for social sanity in a violence-prone world."[15] What if both the black theologian and the Jewish scholar-mystic are correct? What if the way that King was exploring is indeed vital to the future of our nation and our world? For scholars, citizens, or celebrants to forget the real man and his deepest implications would be not only faithless, but also suicidal. For in the light of the news that inundates us every day, where else do we go from here to make a better world?

CHAPTER 5

THE LAND BEYOND

Reflections on King's
"Beyond Vietnam" Speech

Somehow Martin King refuses to die within us, among us. Many years after it was delivered in 1967, his historic Riverside Church speech, "Beyond Vietnam," reappears and thrusts upon us a King we had largely chosen to forget. Even now it would be tempting to take this cry from the heart of a driven, searching, magnificent brother and file it away as a document for museums and other honorable places.

But neither the fiery signals rising from some of our latest potential Vietnams in Central America, South Africa, or the Middle East, nor the mounting anguish of the betrayed and disinherited of our own land will allow us to escape the unresolved issues of the past or avoid the costly and accurate vision of our comrade in the faith. The speech not only requires us to struggle once more with the meaning of King, but it also presses us to wrestle, as he did, with all of the tangled, bloody, and glorious meaning of our nation (and ourselves), its purposes (and our own), its direction (and our own), its hope (and our own).

Recently the name of Martin Luther King, Jr., has been in the public arena primarily as the person whose birthday should or should not be a legal holiday. But this rather smoothed-off, respectable national hero is not the King of "Beyond Vietnam." Those who have, with all the best and most understandable intentions, pressed for King's birthday as an official holiday, seem to have enshrined the King of 1963. In a way, that is a more comfortable image for us all: the triumphant King of the March on Washington, calling a nation and a world to a magnificent dream of human solidarity.

But all that was before the assassins' bombs ripped out the life of the Sunday school children in Birmingham, before the fires of rebellion scourged the Northern cities and moved King into Chicago, before the cry of Black Power was raised, before courageous and radical spokespersons like Malcolm X and the leaders of the Student Nonviolent Coordinating Committee (SNCC) had begun to testify against the steadily rising tide of destructive U.S. imperialism in Vietnam, before King decided to break what he called the silence of betrayal and speak his own truth concerning his nation's role in Vietnam and in all the world's nonwhite revolutionary struggles.

Sometimes we wish to forget that by April 1967, King was a beleaguered public figure. He had refused to join the fearful litany of condemnation mounted by the civil rights establishment against the militant demands for black power, and for that he was fiercely attacked by moderates and liberals. On the other hand, some of the younger black and white radicals seemed to think that their best contributions to revolution were measured by the harshness of their criticism of King's nonviolence and "moderation."

At the same time, he had also begun to be heard publicly as a critic of the war in Vietnam, and from within the black community and among the ranks of many of its self-proclaimed white allies, King was bitterly rebuked for taking on the issue of the war. Some called it a diversion from the issue of black rights. Others feared the terrible rage of Lyndon Johnson who brooked no opposition (certainly not from black Martin Luther King!) to his destructive policies.

Some members of King's own Southern Christian Leadership Conference (SCLC) board of directors opposed his role in the antiwar movement, partly because they had seen the way in which the liberal white allies of the movement had withdrawn financial support from the radicalized young people of SNCC, who dared stand in solidarity with the Vietnamese opponents of America's intervention. The SCLC officials and advisers knew such a fate could, and probably would, befall their organization as well. Of course, other persons—black and white—were simply dead to the movement of history.

In the face of all this, partly because of all this, King persisted, and the Riverside speech—delivered exactly one year before his assassination, was the most notable result of his decision. Immediately the drumbeat of harsh criticism was heightened. It came from many sources, including such black stalwarts as Jackie Robinson, Roy Wilkins, Whitney Young, and Carl Rowan.

On the white side, one typical response emerged from the liberal/paternal editorial pages of the *Washington Post.* There the reaction to "Beyond Vietnam" was that King had uttered "bitter and damaging allegations and inferences that he did not and could not document," and had thereby "done a grave injury to those who are his natural allies. . . ." It was the *Post*'s considered judgment that "many who have listened to him with respect will never again accord him the same confidence. He has diminished his usefulness to his cause, to his country, and to his people."

(Later, of course, the *Post* and many other similarly well-informed journals would carry on their own front pages, direct from government files, all the documentation for King's condemnation of America's role that he had not bothered to supply. And history will yet judge the "usefulness" of King to the cause of humanity and to the redemption of his nation and "his people.")

Whatever the judgment of others might be, by April 1967, King had clearly decided that the federal government was not among his "natural allies." He knew that its leadership and several of its agencies had been carrying on an insidious campaign to subvert and discredit him personally, and he was well aware that they perceived the mounting force of black Northern militancy as a serious threat whose power and direction they could neither predict nor control.

Moreover, when King looked at Vietnam, and beyond, he felt that he had no choice but to identify his own government as the

In April 1967 King marches in anti-Vietnam War demonstration with Dr. Benjamin Spock and Msgr. Charles C. Rice.

"greatest purveyor of violence in the world." For he was convinced that his vocation as a minister of Christ and his broader, deeper calling as a child of the loving God of the universe meant that he must cry out against America's wanton destruction of the lives of the poor in Vietnam (both Vietnamese people and American soldiers) and the betrayal of the hopes of the poor at home. This was one of the major themes of the Riverside speech.

In addition, King was prepared by then to urge all Americans to seek out their own highest possible level of protest and resistance against their government's role in Southeast Asia. He was even ready to take on the dangerous issue of calling for all draft-age persons, including normally exempt clergy and poorly informed black and poor people, who opposed the war to declare themselves conscientious objectors. (King was deeply troubled by the fact that the black church lagged so far behind in its responsibility to teach its young people about the choice of conscientious objection as a logical Christian alternative to the military.)

Even more important, King insisted that we look "beyond Vietnam." Indeed, for our purposes, in our times, that may have been the most significant contribution of his speech, of the last years of his life—this public wrestling with the role of America in the world, this agonized calling of his "beloved nation" away from its destructive, inhumane choices, toward its own best truth.

As King saw it, in our overseas relationships, our nation had chosen to be "on the wrong side of a world revolution." And at home, "a nation that continues year after year to spend more money on military defense than on programs of social uplift is approaching spiritual death." (Of course, King was simply the best known of many persons who were pressing that concern. As early as the 1940s, W.E.B. Du Bois had predicted that this country must choose to develop greater democracy and support for socialist alternatives at home and abroad or "descend into military fascism which will kill all dreams of democracy.")

For King, in the light of such national and international realities, there was no humane alternative for America save revolution—nonviolent revolution to be sure, but revolution nevertheless. In "Beyond Vietnam" he spoke primarily of the urgent need for a "revolution in values . . . a significant and profound change in American life and policy," but he also made it clear that there could be no change in people's values that was not tied to radical change in the structures of their society.

If we desire greater clarity concerning King's approach to these crucial issues in his last months, then his Riverside speech must be read in the context of at least two other readily available documents. One is his sermon/essay, "Nonviolence and Social Change," which appeared in the posthumously published collection of his writings, *The Trumpet of Conscience.* The second is David Garrow's carefully researched book, *The FBI and Martin Luther King, Jr.,* especially his chapters, "The Informant" and "The Radical Challenge of Martin King."

In these documents we are reminded that by the end of 1967, King himself had moved beyond a narrow approach to the war in Vietnam and had long before rejected a single narrow focus on black rights in the United States. By the end of that crucial year, King was openly declaring that "the dispossessed of this nation— the poor, both white and Negro—live in a cruelly unjust society. They must organize a revolution against that injustice, not against the lives of . . . their fellow citizens, but against the structures through which the society is refusing . . . to lift the load of poverty."

By then he was vaguely but courageously advocating campaigns of "massive civil disobedience . . . to compel unwilling federal authorities to yield to the mandates of justice." Originally that was supposed to be the purpose of the Poor People's Campaign: the opening of a nationwide movement of "massive civil disobedience" on behalf of radical, humanizing change in America.

Moreover, by the end of 1967, King was looking at the anti-imperialist movements of Latin America and declaring that "so many of Latin America's problems have roots in the United States of America that we need to form a solid united movement, nonviolently conceived and carried through. . . ." For he was convinced that "Americans must help their nation repent of her modern economic imperialism."

Whether we want him or not, this is the King who refuses to die within us, among us. This is the King who was under constant covert surveillance by the FBI and other organs of the federal government, whose organization was infiltrated by at least one FBI informer. This is the King our government feared. It was this King of whom David Garrow could accurately say, "In the last twelve months of his life, King represented a far greater political threat to the reigning American government than he ever had before." (Therefore, this is the King whose assassination was surely not the work of some lone and unabetted white racist criminal.)

For this Martin Luther King, Jr., there seemed by 1967 to be only two authentic alternatives available to those compassionate children of God who deeply sensed their vocation and their ultimate identity, and who at the same time lived as citizens of this destructive, antirevolutionary, but not hopeless, nation: either we could confine ourselves to courageous fighting of brush fires around the nation and across the world, until the last terrible fire destroyed us all, or we could dedicate ourselves to what he called "the long and bitter—but beautiful—struggle for a new world," beginning with the revolutionary transformation of America. Of course, King was enough of a dialectician to know that such a larger commitment would not end our work in the brush-fire brigade, but it would place that work in context and give us a larger task, a deeper purpose, a greater hope to which we might set ourselves.

This sense of revolutionary vocation did not come easily to King. It was not the life for which he once had thought he was preparing. The relatively secure joint career of pastor and college professor had seemed an attractive possibility while he worked on his doctoral studies. But by 1967 he saw no escape from God's movement in history, and its urgent summons to a life of creative insecurity. So, with much fear and trembling, he answered the call, saying essentially, fittingly, "I can do no other."

Now, in the light of our nation's current realities, what shall *we* do with this King who saw many years ago that "we can't solve our problems . . . until there is a radical redistribution of economic and political power" in the United States? How shall we grapple with the vision of this man who knew that he was engaged in "much more than a struggle for the rights of Negroes," who realized that the black movement was "forcing America to face all its interrelated flaws—racism, poverty, militarism, and materialism." King said that the black freedom struggle was "exposing the evils that are deeply rooted in the whole structure of our society. It reveals systemic rather than superficial flaws and suggests that radical reconstruction of society itself is the real issue to be faced."

Of course, at our best we know that the fundamental question is not what we shall do with King, but what we shall do with ourselves, with our nation, with our children, with our poor, with our sick, with our fears, with our joblessness, with our system of economic injustice and military destructiveness. What shall we do with the poisons in our food, in our air, in our water, in our hearts? What shall we do with our broken hope in one traditional political party or another, in one leader or another, in one worn-out, no-longer-radical, "radical" solution after another? In other words, the question focuses into one critical issue. Now, so many years after Riverside, after Memphis, after the fall of Saigon, after the time of Reagan and company, are we prepared to go beyond Central America, to face what King called "the real issue . . . the radical reconstruction of American society itself"?

Instead of enshrining him as a plastic, powerless hero of a nation that is not yet open to the coming of his vision, is it possible that those of us who want to be open must now sense our call to a different task? Is it possible that our best vocation begins as we examine with utmost seriousness his last, most radical hopes, and ponder what they mean for our lives? Is it possible that the state of our nation and our world now demands that we who consider ourselves part of King's company of experimenters with truth must commit ourselves to move with him, to press forward beyond him toward that fundamental transformation of ourselves and of America that is even more necessary in these days than ever before?

A variety of groups, networks, organizations, and fledgling movements are giving themselves to this urgent search for a radically transformed America, a search that begins with the commitment to personal transformation. They are exploring paths that take us beyond the sometimes war-weary categories of the most valiant Marxist/socialist/revolutionary visions and experiences of the past. They are seeking to understand the profoundly American ingredients of the revolution that we need, that our children must have. Among other things, they are asking questions concerning the public implications of our popular quest for personal self-discovery, about the meaning of responsible American citizenship in our current age.

Ultimately, of course, each of us who has been touched most directly by the significant work of such organizations and by the meaning of King must decide what our responses will be. As we work toward such decisions perhaps it is more than naive optimism to sense that Ronald Reagan and the forces of reaction and fear that he seems to represent are not the beginning of something new in the United States but the danger-filled end of the line for a failing culture.

Perhaps the time is now ripe to begin to envision a new network, a new gathering of forces, a new scattered/gathered community based on a profoundly humane, inclusively religious foundation. Perhaps it is past time for us to recognize all the intimations of new life that are already springing up within the shaken foundations of our nation. Perhaps we are part of the skin-shedding time that cannot be turned back.

King's movement beyond Vietnam and our current actions to break the bondage of cynicism, privatism, and despair may encourage us to move beyond the 1970s and 80s. For instance, we may begin to recognize that we can take all of the insights of personal transformation that have come out of our latest ongoing spiritual renascence and integrate them with a commitment to the radical re-creation of our nation. Constantly sensing new connections, we may find creative ways to share our insurgent hope for life and renewal and justice and peace with our sisters and brothers of every land, especially with those who are now ground down into the dirt, often to support our U.S. standard of

living. We may listen to them, learn from them, hearing their
voices from the base communities of Latin America, from the
freedom churches of South Africa, from the bombed-out villages
of the Middle East.

We have no clear models for doing all this, but there are inspi-
rations everywhere, in Asia, Africa, Latin America, in our land,
and in the whisper roaring of the wind and the dancing rhythms
of the waters. We have no models for the new American society,
but we know it must be. We know it must build our humanity and
steadily diminish the power of the antihuman forces of greed,
exploitation, fear, and all ideas of supremacy based on race, class,
gender, or genes. It must hear the words of King ("The choice is
between nonviolence and nonexistence") and eschew all weapons of military destruction, all institutions whose lives are based
on the assumptions that human problems can be solved by military force, by threats of annihilation.

Something within us (and we trust our intuition more fully in
these times of feminine power) tells us that whatever the developing shape of our new society it must be structured so as to make
the resources of Mother Earth available to all of her children, in as
just and equitable a way as is possible. Somehow we know that our
new direction must develop all our best capacities for creative self-
government and cooperation.

It must create new forms and content for the education of our
people toward their highest human capacities. It must put as
many of us as possible in direct touch with the land and its
teaching, nurturing forces. It must change our total relationship
to the people of the land all over the world, bring us into a new
sense of solidarity rather than exploitation in our dealings with
the raw-materials producers of the earth.

Indeed, the movement that we shall take toward a new society
must be such that it will bring us into solidarity with all who seek
for the gift of their land, who seek for food for their children,
who attempt to break the combination of despoiling, exploiting
classes and institutions everywhere. Then, returning to the source,
always, necessarily, our struggle must be such that it opens us to a

new sense of ourselves, of our humanity, of our oneness with the created universe and its creator spirit.

To organize toward such a radical reconstruction of America and ourselves, to work for such a vision, to struggle for such a vindication of the best hopes of the Kings and the A.J. Mustes, the Fannie Lou Hamers and the Randy Blackwells, the Dorothy Days and the Amzie Moores, the Clarence Jordans, the Paul Robesons, and the Thomas Mertons of this land—that task will take all the creativity, all the courage, all the life force we can give. To be faithful to itself, our work will certainly demand that we move beyond King's last, uncertain vision of the Poor People's Campaign and truly honor him with audacious, creative thinking and organizing toward that which has never yet existed: a spiritually based, life-giving revolution, seeking for the fundamental reordering of the institutions of society in the world's most technologically organized, militarily equipped, and materialistically oriented society.

Moreover, for King, for ourselves, for our children, we are challenged by his vision to leap even further, to conceive of such a revolution based essentially on the commitment to new life through nonviolence, noncooperation, massive civil disobedience, and love. It is an awesome responsibility, but does our God-given humanity leave us with any other authentic choice at this moment in history?

Lest there be any misunderstanding, one more word needs to be said. The movement with King beyond Vietnam, beyond El Salvador, even beyond South Africa, does not mean that we move away from any of the concrete struggles that have been represented by those places. It surely does not mean that we lessen our commitment to the daily quests for justice in our own society on behalf of all those who are continually suffering attacks from the bastions of privilege and illegitimate power and authority. Rather, our commitment to the revolutionary transformation of ourselves and of American society gives us a context, a sense of direction. For as we engage in the dialectical exchange between daily struggles and larger vision, we may be reminded of certain basic realities. One of them is that our ultimate goal can no longer be seen as that of pressing the government of our nation for a change of its policies. Indeed, it cannot even be simply a goal of putting different men or women in the governmental structures and institutions that we now know.

Rather, our vision must be set toward creating and legitimating a new kind of government, one which will call forth our own best self-governing gifts as persons and communities, one which will surely break the unholy, traditional governmental alliances with militarism, racism, sexism, and economic imperialism, one which will move us insistently beyond the nationalism of our immaturity toward the recognition of our true global kinship.

Beyond Vietnam, beyond Memphis, beyond protest of every kind lies the unknown. And yet something within us knows the land for which we seek, the community that will nurture our humanity, the radically humanized America. At various moments in the heat of the struggles of the last quarter century we glimpsed it, felt it, knew it could be. (Perhaps it exists most vividly in the midst of struggle for that which is yet to be.) Now we dare not betray that vision.

For beyond Vietnam lies the reality that we who share the best hopes and vision of King are essentially citizens of a nation that does not yet exist. And yet it does, it must, beginning in us. It is a nation that we must create, all of us, out of all the terrors and beauties of our history and our blood, out of all the dreams and wailings of our forebears, for all the colors and callings of our children.

Beyond Vietnam, beyond Central America, beyond the United States that we now know, beyond the women and men that we now are, we are called to create a new reality. Because King opened so much and had so much opened for him within the vortex of the black freedom movement, because his Riverside speech offers such a summons to us, perhaps it would be good to allow a poetic expression of that freedom movement to extend the final call to all who will hear, to all who will love, to all who will struggle, to all who will risk, to all who will dare to move forward

beyond cynicism, privatism, fear, and the dark night of despair
toward the coming of the morning:

> Into your palm I place the ashes
> Into your palm are the ashes of your
>   people
> burnt in the Alabama night
> Into your hand that holds your babies
> into your palm that feeds your infants
> into your palm that holds the work tools
> I place the ashes of your brother and your
>   sister
> I place the ashes of your father and your
>   mother
> here are the ashes of your husbands and
>   your wives
> Take the ashes of your nation
> and create the cement to build again
> Create the spirits to move again
> Take this soul dust and begin again.
>
> Ed Bullins, *Creation Spell*

CHAPTER 6

WE MUST KEEP GOING

It was March 25, 1968. The spring had just begun, and no one knew how late it was, how short the time, for him, for us. In the midst of a cruelly demanding schedule, Martin Luther King, Jr., had flown to upstate New York to speak to a gathering of Jewish rabbis. He was introduced to the group by Dr. Abraham Joshua Heschel, one of the great teachers of that faith community.

Heschel, the bearded, white-haired mystic, who was also scholar and activist, had long been deeply obsessed by the call for compassionate justice which rises relentlessly from the scriptures of Jews and Christians. More than once he had responded to the divine imperative by marching at the side of his friend and leader, the black Christian prophet of the nonviolent freedom struggle. So he was a natural choice to present King to the Rabbinical Assembly.

At the heart of Heschel's introduction was a proclamation and a challenge that could not be contained by time, place, or people. For on that Monday afternoon, just ten days before the long-traveling assassin's bullet finally found Martin King, Abraham Heschel announced,

> Martin Luther King, Jr., is a voice, a vision, and a way. I call upon every Jew to harken to his voice, to share his vision, to follow in his way. The whole future of America will depend on the impact and influence of Dr. King.

Now, almost twenty years later, it is tempting to believe that we Americans—Jews and Gentiles alike—have a ready response to

A. Massalek/Maryknoll

King addressing anti-war rally in New York City.

Heschel's stirring call. Now that King seems safely dead, now that he has been properly installed in the national pantheon—to the accompaniment of military bands, with the U.S. Marine Corps chorus singing "We Shall Overcome," and the cadenced marching of the armed forces color guards—we think we know the man's impact and influence. Didn't President Reagan sign a bill authorizing a national holiday honoring this teacher of nonviolence (shortly after the president had sent the comrades of the singers and musicians to carry out an armed attack on Grenada, one of the smallest countries in the world)? And didn't Vice-President Bush go to Atlanta to help inaugurate the King national holiday in January 1986 (presumably taking time off from his general oversight of the murderous Nicaraguan counterrevolutionary forces who were being brutally manipulated in this government's cynical attempt to destroy what was one of the most hopeful revolutions for the poor in the Americas)?

And didn't Coca-Cola make available one of its corporate jets to fly King family members and friends from one celebration to another—perhaps hoping that the sounds of the engines would drown out all the cries of the black children being shot down in South Africa, a place where "things go better" for Coke's stockholders? And aren't there Martin Luther King, Jr., celebrations at U.S. military installations all over the world (celebrations where King's unrelenting condemnation of American militarism and his call for conscientious objectors are rarely heard)? What more impact and influence could we want? Aren't school children in every state of the nation now taught that "Dr. King loved everybody" (and who answers them, in what stumbling words, when they ask if such love includes Russians, Libyans, and Sandinista leaders—and all the billions of human beings who are the actual targets and potential victims of America's perilously poised nuclear weapons)?

Even those of us who feel drawn to King—and who now seek to stand as far as possible from the cruel ironies of such national hero-making—are not immune to amnesia. Guarding against self-righteousness, watching a nation try to whittle a rough and ragged-edged giant down to smooth and manageable size, we too may need to see and hear Heschel and King again. Perhaps the passage of time has blunted, or romanticized, our own memory. Perhaps distance has blurred our vision, the strange, bewildering times of the 1970s and 1980s confused our sense of King's voice, his vision, his way. Perhaps—and this is even more likely—each generation must forge its own understanding of King's meaning, must determine and demonstrate the power of his impact and influence for our own lives. Perhaps that is the way the whole future of America is being wrought.

If that is the case, and I think it is, then we have lately been granted some very helpful resources for our own revisioning of the paradoxical national hero and his significance for our time, his meaning for our lives. One is a helpful collection of some of King's important speeches, sermons, interviews, and articles, gathered in a hefty work called *Testament of Hope*, edited by James Melvin Washington. The second tool is the latest and most meticulously researched biography of King, *Bearing the Cross*, by David Garrow (from which most of the King quotes in this article have come). Finally, there is "Eyes on the Prize," a powerful series of documentary films aired in 1987 on the PBS national network.

Making full use of such resources, those of us who sense some new impulse to respond to Heschel's challenge, others who have long been committed to the building of a compassionate society, as well as younger persons who are just beginning to search out the focus of their own lives—all of us—may explore the territory, re-vision the hero, consider the challenge anew. This is our chance to be sure that we have really seen the Martin King who stood in the presence of the rabbis. Plumbing collective memory, probing images and documents, we may recollect at the deepest levels of our being the sound and message of his voice, the shape and texture of his vision, gain some new purchase on the hard, uncharted vectors of his way. Only then may it be possible to absorb and respond to the real significance of Abraham Heschel's last words: "The whole future of America will depend on the impact and influence of Dr. King."

To see King as he was in those last weeks of his life, even at the simplest levels of our perception, is to see an exhausted, hard-pressed, at times beleaguered-looking brother (didn't Malcolm look that way in his last days?), far older than the thirty-nine years of his life, often saying, "I'm tired now, I've been in this thing thirteen years and now I'm really tired." All around him we hear voices filled with accusation, fear, hostility, and disdain, calling him "traitor," "stupid," "misleading," "provocative," "communist dupe";—and "Martin Loser King." To see him as he was then is to see the disappointment in his eyes as he shared "his feeling that his closest friends and assistants were failing to stand by him in his hour of greatest need." Making use of Garrow's invaluable research in government files, we look closely and recognize the now too-familiar sight of King's own government at work against him, especially through "our" FBI, subverting, planting spies, playing "dirty tricks," writing anonymous letters, seeking to break and destroy the great believer in America's best truths, justifying it all in J. Edgar Hoover's words: ". . . it is clear that [King] is an instrument in the hands of subversive forces seeking to undermine our nation." In the presence of that lying assumption, no holds were barred. None. To look carefully into King's last weeks, then, is to see darkness, both the creative and the perilous darkness of the wilderness.

Is this what Heschel meant by King's "way," this dangerous, uncharted, and often lonely path? And how did he (we?) get here? What was the road to the wilderness? Which paths led out from that bright and sunny day of August 1963—less than five years earlier? There he seemed to be celebrated by a nation, a world, surrounded by the hundreds of thousands who represented the hosts of Americans committed to his light-filled dream. There he held forth the vision of black and white children of God, holding hands, keeping faith, working for freedom. That has been our primary image of him, our primary hope for him, and for ourselves. How do you get to the wilderness from there?

Somehow we have forgotten that the movement from adulation to wilderness is not a new one for those children of the light who are consumed by a hunger and thirst for righteousness. Somehow, we have frozen the frame of the smiling, victorious hero, locked in the magnificent voice proclaiming the compelling dream; but neither the hero nor his voice, neither the vision nor the way, could be held captive, static, manageable. That was part of King's power. And what we discover through close and painful attention is that the hero, the voice, the vision and the way continued to develop, to deepen, to expand, to burst beyond the limits that America had set for him—that he had once set for himself. Rabbi Heschel, friend and follower, saw that volatile, creative transformation at work, and dared beckon us toward the dangerous but necessary fellowship of hope.

Now, for those of us who wish to explore King's movement toward the cutting edges, toward the radical depths, Garrow's work serves us well. For he follows the trail with meticulous care, tracking many (surely not all) of the deep places, revealing the pitfalls, offering much material for serious thought, perhaps even for inspiration. For example, it is clear that King knew better than many of his family, associates, and friends that there was no permanent residence for him on the plains of good will. For even as we were still warming in the glow of the March on Washington, four young girls, and many millions vicariously with them, felt all the murderous, death-filled power of white America's racial hatred when the bomb exploded in Birmingham's 16th Street Baptist Church. So, short weeks after the rendezvous in the sun, King was called into the darkness to preach the funeral service for three of the four Sunday school girls whose lives had been blasted away. Afterwards he claimed that this was the point when his late summer's dream had begun to turn into a nightmare; but there in the presence of mourning and rage King said what he knew he had to say, what he wanted to believe, "The innocent blood of these little girls may well serve as the redemptive force that will bring new light on this dark city."

Deep within him he wondered if there was any hope, any light, for this nation. And perhaps at deeper levels still he had to face himself with the knowledge that the bomb was a direct response to the powerful, confrontational movement he had helped to lead, and that the children were stricken soldiers in that nonviolent army of hope. (At that level, could he hear the freedom song: "We are soldiers/in the Army/We have to fight/Although we have to cry/We have to hold up the freedom banner/We have to hold it up until we die. . . ."?) So when he sat with Coretta in November 1963, and watched the tragic drama of Dallas being acted out, it was not surprising that King should say, quietly, painfully, against his wife's objections, "I don't think I'm going to live to reach forty. . . . This is such a sick society."

To miss that part of the voice, the vision, and the way is to miss King. For the violence of American society and the steady movement of the collectively created assassin's bullet were always with him, not like a heavy burden most of the time, but like a persistent presence to be reckoned with as he counted the costs. King felt this when he went into Mississippi in the summer of 1964 and saw the angry, mournful eyes of the black and white volunteers, remembering their murdered comrades in the freedom army. Later that year he reminded the world that such deaths were part of the price all the nonviolent freedom fighters had paid for his—and their—Nobel Peace Prize. The sadness of the eyes, the symbol of the honor, the cost of it all, the long road he had already traveled beyond the March on Washington—these were part of the painfully expanding vision of Martin Luther King.

Of course, King was also opened, deepened, by challenges, like the one presented by that other black prince, Malcolm X —Al Hajj Malik El Shabazz. For Malcolm was a child of the black urban North, denizen of its cities, survivor of its terrors, testimony to the power of the redeeming spirit. Disciplined by prison and by the Nation of Islam, renewed by internal struggle and the blessings of Allah, filled with a tough, compassionate love, "He became much more than there was time for him to be." Somehow, though, there was a fascinating dialectic at work, and near the end, in spite of (or because of) all the hard words he had once had for King, Malcolm ultimately knew himself as brother to his Southern-born companion in the search for the truth of America. So, early in February 1965, he came to Selma, Alabama, partly to establish new, more cooperative contacts with King. Then, late in February, while the links were still of spirit alone, he was assassinated, before he was forty. (Was there any connection between the Southern journey and the Northern bullets?)

The death of Malcolm released a great and rising stream of black consciousness into the freedom movement, perhaps opening for King the legacy of the Muslim brother's deep concern for the black outsiders, for the urban poor, for the millions of black men and women whose prisons were both with and without walls, whose jailers were all the keepers of the nation's economic, political, and religious status quo. Perhaps Malcolm's unyielding life and voice became part of King's own harshening tone, strengthened his magnificent compassion, helped sensitize his already deepening concern for the children of poverty, turned the younger brother's face and heart more firmly toward the wounded outcries from the North.

For even as he marched from Selma to Montgomery in the spring of 1965, gathering the forces of good will, attracting the bearers of death—even as he moved toward his past and his future on that last great pilgrimage of the traditional Southern-based freedom movement, King had already experienced the call of the North, of the cities, of the poor. There in Montgomery, his way led far beyond that older base of operations, beyond the best dreams of his past. The change was evident in the closing words of his speech to the marchers and their companions, delivered that day in early spring on the steps of the capitol of the Old Confederacy, proclaimed in sight of Dexter Avenue Baptist Church, where he had begun his full-time pastoral ministry just eleven years before. To the thousands who had gathered to end the march and challenge Alabama and America to do justice, King made clear that the challenge was broader and deeper than the voting rights bill which had been the focus of their march. He said,

We are on the move now. The burning of our churches will not deter us. We are on the move now. The bombing of our homes will not dissuade us. We are on the move now. The beating and killing of our clergymen and young people will not divert us. We are on the move now. . . . We are moving to the land of freedom. . . . Let us therefore continue our triumph and march to the realization of the American dream.

King, himself, was moving. And it was revealing to hear his definition of what it meant to realize "the American dream" in 1965. He said,

Let us march on segregated housing, until every ghetto of social and economic depression dissolves and Negroes and whites live side by side in decent, safe and sanitary housing. Let us march on segregated schools until every vestige of segregated and inferior education becomes a thing of the past and Negroes and whites study side by side in the socially healing context of the classroom. Let us march on poverty, until no American parent has to skip a meal so that their children may [eat], until no starved man walks the streets of our cities and towns in search of jobs that do not exist.

These were the issues increasingly at the center of his agenda —along with voting rights. King knew that it was a costly movement, a long road. For those who considered taking the way, he made it clear that no one could expect any prearranged maps or guideposts. "The road ahead is not altogether a smooth one," he said. "There are no broad highways to lead us easily and inevitably to quick solutions." Nevertheless, whatever else was unclear for King, one thing seemed absolutely certain, and he declared it to the gathered throng: "We must keep going."

He was on his way, moving beyond his relatively secure and familiar Southern Christian base, responding to the volatile secular cities of the North. After another hard-fought Southern victory in St. Augustine, Florida, in the summer of 1965, King's path led to Watts, a lower-middle-class black community in the midst of Los Angeles's sprawling metropolis. In the second week of August, it had exploded in black fire and rage. Sparked by the almost ritualized arrogant violence of white police against black people, the incendiary rebellion brought thousands of National Guardsmen into the area, left more than thirty black people dead, and drew King into the arena.

There in Watts, he saw much that affected his vision, much that he would see again in the "hot summers" of the North: the smouldering wreckage of the neighborhood; the strange claim of victory announced amid the rubble by young black men who looked at the rest of the uncaring country and said, "We made them pay attention"; the sense of desolation (and some stubborn pride) in the devastated black community; the fear, ignorance, and insensitivity among many whites, and too many middle-class black folk. Seeing, feeling these things, King tried to speak for an angry, distressed people who he said had "been bypassed by the progress of the past decade" in the South. Indeed, the sensitive black leader dared to say that the uprising was "a class revolt of under-privileged against privileged." In such a setting, King claimed, "major economic reforms" were urgently needed, "a massive economic program . . . to give the people in the ghetto a stake in the country." From then until the coming of the bullet, King did not cease trying to speak, to express the hopes, to pay attention to the needs and deep angers of the poor.

But the act of speaking was never enough attention for King. As Heschel said, this justice-obsessed man was a way, was constantly in movement, always leaving the easily managed, but totally inadequate freeze frames of "great orator," or "civil rights leader." Indeed, by the winter of 1966, Martin King had clearly turned the focus of his life and his organization from the earlier battle grounds of the South to the North, especially to Chicago.

They chose that machine-ridden, highly segregated city, King said, because "Chicago represents all the problems that you can find in the major urban areas of our country. . . . If we can break the system in Chicago, it can be broken anywhere in the country." They were right, but that did not mean they were prepared.

In Chicago, King and the Southern Christian Leadership Conference had to face aspects of the struggle for freedom and justice which had not engaged them so fully before. They met the problems of segregated neighborhoods and often dilapidated housing, owned by irresponsible, profit-hungry landlords, including black ones. Then, there were the hard realities of segregated underfinanced schools that were not providing for the needs of the black children and youth who cried out so desperately for skilled, compassionate attention and who required serious financial commitment. King and his staff encountered the harsh dilemma of rising unemployment and underemployment as it eroded the life of the black community. In Chicago, all of this was placed against the background of a highly organized, white-controlled political machine, based on corruption, coercion, and great political skills. It was, moreover, a machine that offered just enough patronage to certain black political operatives and office holders to make the scene far more racially complicated than in the South.

Nevertheless, driven by a combination of compassion, commitment to the poor, and stubborn foolhardiness, King moved in. By the end of January 1966, he had established a partly real, partly symbolic, but always seriously intentional residence at 1550 S. Hamlin, in the heart of the broken and exploited Lawndale black community. This was his part-time residence, this was SCLC's base for organizing with their Chicago allies. Far from the Mall in Washington, this was part of the new vision and the new way. Indeed, Chicago (and the cities of the North in general) helped to deepen the transformation already at work in Martin King. Now his voice was heard raising issues of class, wealth, and economic injustice far more frequently than before. (He had always been conscious of such things, but the move to the North brought them vividly alive.) Now he spoke against "our vicious class systems" in America, and told his Ebenezer Church congregation, "If our economic system is to survive, there has to be a better distribution of wealth . . . we can't have a system where some people live in superfluous, inordinate wealth, while others live in abject, deadening poverty." From now on, he said, the movement would take on "basic class issues between the privileged and the underprivileged."

This was the voice and the vision of Martin Luther King, Jr., now being sharpened, chastened, focused by the realities of poverty, dispossession, legal exploitation, and white self-righteousness in the North. Ultimately, the Chicago experience, the challenge of the exploding cities and all their people, led him to declare,

> I choose to identify with the underprivileged. I choose to identify with the poor. I choose to give my life for the hungry. I choose to give my life for those who have been left out of the sunlight of opportunity. I choose to live for and with those who find themselves seeing life as a long and desolate corridor with no exit sign. This is the way I'm going. If it means suffering a little bit, I'm going that way. If it means sacrificing, I'm going that way. If it means dying for them, I'm going that way, because I heard a voice saying, "Do something for others."

This was more than oratory and civil rights. It was commitment rising from the depths of experience, annealed through hard, often unsuccessful experiments at challenging Mayor Daley's machine in Chicago. The voice was developing out of King's periodic visits into the apartments of poor families in his adopted city and elsewhere, feeling, seeing, smelling the inhuman injustice to which these vulnerable Americans were being subjected in their dilapidated dwellings, all for the sake of profit. The voice grew as he grappled with an inexperienced, inadequate, and too often undisciplined staff to discover the ways of organizing the poor, of entering into their organizing of themselves. Its power was reinforced by his long conversations with the black gang leaders of Chicago and Cleveland, where he did much listening and much learning about what it was like to grow up black, poor, politically exploited, and educationally ignored in a city. The voice was the product of increased conversation in the search for common ground with those who held other views in the black community of struggle, such as Elijah Muhammad, leader of the Chicago-based Nation of Islam. Of course, King's voice was also shaped by his attempts to march with hundreds of black and white co-workers into the heart of Chicago's racially segregated and fearfully hostile white communities. It came out of his experience of being stoned, and hearing himself say, again, "If some of us have to die, then we will die."

Surely it is understandable if we choose to forget so disturbing and imperative a voice, a vision, a way. They are not easy to claim in our undisciplined, self-indulgent culture. Indeed, King often found it hard to accept his own rigorous sense of calling, and in the midst of Chicago's harsh, demanding, and frustrating struggles, he was heard to say more than once:

> I'm tired of marching for something that should have been mine at first. . . . I'm tired of the tensions surrounding our days. . . . I'm tired of living every day under the threat of death. I have no martyr complex. I want to live as long as anybody . . . and sometimes I begin to doubt whether I'm going to make it through. I must confess I'm tired. . . . I don't march because I like it, I march because I must.

In essence, then, he was responding to his own earlier call: "We must keep going." That was King's way, to keep going—in spite of personal weaknesses that sometimes cast him into dangerous pitfalls, in spite of many fears. Sometimes, it might have been better had he stopped to reflect, to be still. Sometimes he tried, for short times. But mostly he kept going. And in Chicago, in all of the cities of the North, part of what drove him on was the relentless search for a new manifestation of the nonviolence which was at the bedrock of his vision of social change. In that urban fortress, he began his search for a way to escalate the Southern-shaped tactics of nonviolent resistance in ways that would do justice to the higher energy, greater rage, and greater complexity of Northern urban settings. So, in the midst of the Chicago campaign, King spoke of finding some kind of direct action "that avoids violence, but becomes militant and extreme enough to disrupt the flow of a city." Partly demonstrating his unfailing sense of humor, partly displaying his search for a new way, at one point in the struggle he speculated about such action, saying, "I know it will be rough on them when they have to get 200 people off the Dan Ryan [Expressway], but the only thing I can tell them is, which do you prefer, this or a riot?" He was groping, suggesting: "If 100,000 Negroes march in a major city to a strategic location, they will make municipal operations difficult to conduct . . . and they will repeat this action daily, if necessary. . . ."

King never had the chance to experiment with his speculations, but the questions were—and are—necessary. What is the mass disciplined action needed to attack poverty, exploitation, educational neglect, and abuse? King was searching toward massive civil disobedience, exploring the edges of nonviolent revolutionary action. He was reaching out. At such times, the voice was often uncertain, the vision unclear. In Chicago, operating on unfamiliar ground, working with a sometimes ambivalent staff, moving with so little time, King never worked out that more Northern-based, radical nonviolence. But the search was essential for him—for us. Part of King's sense of urgency had to do with the rising force of violence, not only in the exploding cities of the North, but far more massively and destructively in the actions of this nation's military forces against the peoples of Vietnam.

By the mid-sixties, King was voicing increasingly strong opposition to the American war in Vietnam, often citing his commitment to nonviolence and his vocation as a Christian minister as his primary grounds. For instance, he said, "Violence is as wrong in

A.P./Wideworld

At a prayer vigil against the Vietnam War in February 1968 King joins Rabbi Abraham Heschel (to left) and other religious leaders at Arlington National Cemetery.

Hanoi as it is in Harlem," and to those who criticized his stand against the war, he said, "I am mandated by this calling [to Christian ministry] above every other duty to seek peace among men and to do it even in the face of hysteria and scorn." He told other audiences that if he were younger and subject to the draft he would definitely take a conscientious objector position, and would not accept a military chaplaincy. Eventually, by 1966, he had pressed SCLC to move away from its caution to issue a statement condemning "the immorality and tragic absurdity" of America's role in Indochina.

In this way, King and SCLC had caught up with the earlier, more stridently critical voices of Malcolm X and of the Student Nonviolent Coordinating Committee (SNCC). However, it was not a popular position in those days. Most people in the United States were still unwilling to listen to any serious criticism of their government's position. Indeed, many persons in King's own organization and in the larger civil rights community argued with him about the wisdom of taking a strong, outspoken stand against the war. Some were afraid of incurring the rage of President Johnson, who seemed ever more blindly committed to a cruelly destructive, constantly expanding military solution. Others were simply unable to face the fact that Martin King had become far more than a civil rights leader, and was offering leadership toward the humanizing transformation of the entire nation. (Was that not in keeping with SCLC's original vision: "To redeem the soul of America"?)

For a time, responding to the pressures, King backed off. But the powerful forces of the 1960s allowed no resting places as he continued his journey out beyond the March on Washington, as he sought to shape a new vision of struggle and hope in keeping with his commitment to the poor of America. As so often happened in such a dynamic, expanding social movement, King was pushed forward by unexpected, external events—like the June 1966 shooting of James Meredith in Mississippi. Meredith was the reluctant black hero of the explosive days back in 1962

when his audacity and courage had led to the official desegrega-
tion of the University of Mississippi. Now the unpredictable native
son had chosen to make a solitary walk from the Tennessee
border to the Gulf Coast, a "walk against fear," he called it. But he
was gunned down by a white assailant (though not seriously
wounded) just as he began. The immediate response of the
black freedom and justice organizations was to try to find a way
to continue Meredith's project. What emerged after much debate
was a march that became the occasion for the surfacing of serious
divisions within the movement, focused now on the cry, "We
want Black Power!"

Here was another crucial element in King's transformation.
The seemingly endless and sometimes rancorous debates,
conversations, and arguments among Stokely Carmichael of
SNCC, Floyd McKissick of the Congress of Racial Equality
(CORE), and King—as well as their staffs and supporters—bore
some helpful fruit in the long run. The controversy over Black
Power that was fanned by the media eventually forced King
to explore more deeply than ever before the power of blackness in the Afro-American communities, and the relationship of
black people to social, economic, and political power in
America. So, in the midst of the march, when pushed by
the press, King tried to reconcile—his natural tendency—as well
as to learn. Never rejecting the creative role of white allies, he
said, "the term 'Black Power' does not represent racism. . . . If
we are to solve our problems, we've got to transform our powerlessness into positive and creative power." Later in the summer,
at the annual SCLC convention, King declared that "The
majority of the people in our society are now powerless, and
in no way able to participate in the decision-making. . . . Self-
determination for an oppressed people requires power." By now,
King could also be heard regularly saying such things as, "We
must be proud of our race. We must not be ashamed of being
black. We must believe with all of our hearts that black is as beautiful as any other color."

This was a blacker voice. Now King had been pressed to take up the crucial questions of how a truly multiracial and multicultural society could be built, while encouraging a sense of collective and personal self-worth within the lives of its component peoples. It was only a beginning, but he was making it, exploring the power of blackness. The voice was also sharper, harsher than many persons had heard before. It seemed more forthcoming in its criticism of white people, including (or especially) Northern white people, who had so often felt exempt from King's critical voice. Martin would never call them "Honkey," but there was no escape from his forceful words, announcing that "large segments of white society are more concerned about tranquility and the status quo than about justice and humanity." He spoke the truth sharply, never denying the creative role of white allies in the struggle, he nevertheless announced that "our beloved nation is still a racist country," and insisted that "the vast majority of white Americans are racist." Sometimes he was discouraged enough to conclude that "there aren't enough white persons in our country who are willing to cherish democratic principles over privilege."

This was the voice Rabbi Heschel heard. He certainly knew the voices of prophets. This was the voice he called us to hear. There was, of course, no need to deny the inspiring, moving voice we had heard on the sunlit Mall, but our Jewish teacher was insisting that we allow King to become multivocal in our lives, to break out of our sound chambers, to send rushing, roaring words through our hearts, to test our faith. Indeed, Heschel's call was for us to open ourselves to all the harshness and the urgency that was King at the end. His challenge was for us to recognize, as many searchers for justice have had to, that Fyodor Dostoyevsky was right: "Love in practice is a harsh and dreadful thing compared to love in dreams."

King's way had moved beyond dreams to practice. That movement was not new in his life, for he had been a courageous practitioner when he dared accept the leadership of the Montgomery

Improvement Association in 1955, surely lifetimes behind him now. What was new in the late 1960s was where the movement was going—into the midst of men, women, and children whose lives were often forced against a host of harsh and dreadful walls, with no apparent way out. Reflecting that experience, searching for an exit, his voice could not be untrue to the serrated edges of the people's lives, could not be unfaithful to his vision of the need to organize the poor for confrontation with the powers of oppression. So, by the end of 1966, King was calling SCLC to prepare itself to lead "the poor in a crusade to realize economic and social justice."

For King, it would surely have been easier to embalm his dream, to live on his memory of the Great March, the time of White House sandwiches and convivial gatherings with the president, savoring the occasion for adulation by so many millions. But his basic commitment made that way impossible. Such nostalgic scenes were marvelous for his ego, but they held no promise for the poor. These sisters and brothers needed the bold, courageous practitioners. So King continued to move away from the great celebration, hoping to shape the great challenge on behalf of justice for the nation's dispossessed, beginning with all those he had met on the West Side of Chicago.

But King found that his search for a way to challenge the government and the nation to justice was constantly blocked by the reality of Vietnam. The poor young men of America were being swept up to become victims and executioners in ever larger numbers. The poor of Vietnam were being destroyed physically and culturally. Moreover King knew that all the cruel devastation of an unjust war was draining billions of dollars and lifetimes of energy and creativity out of the nation's potential for dealing with the needs of its own poor people. It was very clear that he would have to take on the war again, confronting it on an even broader front this time, but he wasn't certain about how or when. Then King came across the January 1967 issue of *Ramparts* magazine, dedicated to "The Children of Vietnam," filled with the special, brutal madness that war brings to children, and heightened by all the great American technical skills of destruction. At that point, King decided. He told his staff that "after reading that article, I said to myself, 'Never again will I be silent on an issue that is destroying the soul of our nation and destroying thousands and thousands of little children in Vietnam.'" For all who would hear his voice, he was saying, "I can no longer be cautious about this matter. I feel so deep in my heart that we are so wrong in this country and the time has come for a real prophesy, and I'm willing to go that road."

There he was. On the road, in the way. Now Martin King had broken even more sharply with all the narrow definitions of "civil rights," moving even more deeply into a profound commitment to the poor, and a courageous stand against his own government's ruthless blindness—all on behalf of the soul of his nation and the lives of a poor, nonwhite people. Heschel saw it and called us. Fittingly enough, he was there at Riverside Church in New York City on the night in April 1967 when King poured out his soul, pleading with his nation to come to its senses, accusing his government of being "the greatest purveyor of violence in the world today," calling America to stand with, not against, the revolutions of the poor. (Who knew that night, April 4, that he had precisely one more year to live, that the bullet was closing in?) For King saw the larger context. He had already declared in other places that his "beloved country" was "engaged in a war that seeks to turn the clock of history back and perpetuate white colonialism." Underlying this backwardness, he said, was America's refusal to recognize that "the evils of capitalism are as real as the evils of militarism and evils of racism." Now, in all of his speeches, King's voice was heard calling for what he described as "a revolution in values" in the United States, a struggle to free ourselves from "the triple evils of racism, extreme materialism, and militarism." Without such revolutionary transformation, King said, people of good will in America would end up protesting our nation's new Vietnams all over the world, including Central America.

King's movement to a bold, consistent, prophetic stance frightened and displeased many persons, including some who had
courageously joined his ranks when he was defined as a civil
rights leader. Many of these were having enough difficulties with
Martin's recently developing stance as a committed servant-
leader of the poor. But now to have him in a role that went far
beyond their vision, their commitments, and their courage was
too much. For instance, A. Philip Randolph and Bayard Rustin
backed away—in silence. Roy Wilkins, head of the NAACP, and
Whitney Young of the Urban League made public statements
sharply disassociating themselves from King's position. The
Washington Post represented many other white liberal keepers of
wisdom for black people when it wrote, "He has diminished his
usefulness to his cause, to his country, and to his people." "And
that," they said, "is a great tragedy." In a *Reader's Digest* article, Carl
Rowan, the black syndicated columnist, said that Martin's stance
on Vietnam was "a tragic decision," brought on by "an exagger-
ated appraisal" of his own importance, and by the influence of
communists upon him. This, interestingly enough, was the exact
line being fed to journalists and others by the cynical and fiercely
anticommunist FBI director, J. Edgar Hoover.

To his credit, while King was at times deeply shaken by these
criticisms, he refused to back down. He justified his criticism of
the war not only on the grounds of his peacemaking Christian
ministry and his humanitarian concerns, but because "the war is
hurting us in all of our programs to end slums and to end segregation in schools and to make quality education a reality, to end
the long night of poverty." King made it clear that he was really
pressing for "a radical reordering of our national priorities," one
that would extricate us from Vietnam as quickly as possible—and
save us from any others. For he had said more than once, "A
nation that continues year after year to spend more money on
military defense than on programs of social uplift is approaching
spiritual death."

He would not relent. Too much was at stake. So, late in the
spring of 1967, at the height of the pressure, in the face of attacks

on every side—including some sponsored by the FBI—with his loyalty, sanity, and humility being harshly questioned, King said to his staff, and eventually to everyone else who would listen:

> I want you to know that my mind is made up. I backed up a little when I came out in 1965. My name then wouldn't have been written in any book called *Profiles of Courage*. But now I have decided that I will not be intimidated. I will not be harassed. I will not be silent, and I will be heard.

He was heard, and there were serious negative consequences for SCLC's fund-raising efforts, but he would not be silent. To try to make up for some of the financial losses, King had to move at an even more maddening pace of travel to raise new funds, to work with old contributing friends who were not prepared to support a poor people's prophet. Still, he spoke up, and he was heard—partly because government bugging followed him everywhere. He knew it, and he continued to speak. He was heard, and even though his words against the war and for world peace, with revolutionary justice, are often missing from the current national celebrations, that was his authentic voice. But he had so little time to develop it.

Nevertheless, by the spring of 1967, King's vision of his role in America had steadily expanded and deepened, and he was trying to make sense of its many parts. He told David Halberstam,

> For years I labored with the idea of reforming the existing institutions of the society, a little change here, a little change there. Now I feel quite differently. I think you've got to have a reconstruction of the entire society, a revolution of values.

As the sensitive journalist understood it, King was saying that such a reconstruction would mean, "the possible nationalization of certain industries, a guaranteed annual income, a vast review of foreign investments," and "an attempt to being new life into the cities." Increasingly, in every part of the nation, King was speaking of "a radical redistribution of economic and political power" as the only way to meet the real needs of the poor in America. And he was clearly committed to the meeting of those needs, by the richest country in the world.

Now, with his time being counted in months (did he know?), he continued to reflect on the transformation within himself and in the movement. He saw what we so often fail to see— his movement beyond Montgomery, beyond the March on Washington, beyond Selma. Considering that pilgrimage, that way, he tried to help his SCLC staff understand where they had been, where they still needed to go, where he was surely headed. So he told them, "We have moved from the era of civil rights to the era of human rights." (Was he aware that his brother, Malcolm, had been using the same words shortly before *his* assassination?) In this new era, King announced, "We are called upon to raise certain basic questions about the whole society." Focusing even more sharply on the way they must go, he would go, King continued, saying that up to 1965 "we [had] been in a reform movement. . . . But after Selma and the voting rights bill, we moved into a new era, which must be an era of revolution. I think we must see the great distinction here between a reform movement and a revolutionary movement."

Again, the key difference for him was, "We must recognize that we can't solve our problems now until there is a radical redistribution of economic and political power." At that point, even integration was being more sharply defined as a challenge to the American status quo. King was moving on, declaring that "integration must be seen not merely in aesthetic or romantic terms; it must be seen in political terms. Integration in its true dimensions is shared power."

All through that last full spring and summer, King seemed to be searching, moving, growing, on pilgrimage, often confused and uncertain, but still on his way. He was clearly pressing on, out beyond the familiar hero's place, beyond the older, easier understanding of "integration," which simply called for black people (in relatively small doses) to move gratefully, unquestioningly into the white-owned American "mainstream." By the end of the fall, King's voice, the voice that Heschel heard, was setting forth a jarring theme, declaring, "Something is wrong with capitalism as it now stands in the United States. We are not interested in being integrated into *this* value structure. Power must be relocated. . . ."

His staff heard the voice as it struggled toward new clarity and direction. Its analyses were hard. At their fall retreat, King told them, "The white power structure is still seeking to keep the walls of segregation and inequality substantially intact." Facing that fact, King said he was "not totally optimistic" about the future of their movement for justice, but he made it clear that "I am not ready to accept defeat." The alternative, as he saw it, was to transform the nature of the freedom/justice struggle itself, to recreate the nation. "Negroes . . . must not only formulate a program," he said; "they must fashion new tactics which do not count on government good will, but serve, instead, to compel unwilling authorities to yield to the mandates of justice." Among the goals of such a movement must be a guaranteed annual income and the elimination of slums, King insisted. In that process, he told his staff, it was necessary to keep reminding themselves that their goals had to be transformed, their own values must be changed. "Let us therefore not think of our movement as one that seeks to integrate the Negro into all the existing values of American society," he said. No, he was demanding that "Our economy must become more person-centered than property-centered and profit-centered." Indeed, by now King was regularly saying to the staff that "he didn't believe that capitalism as it was constructed could meet the needs of poor people, and that what we might need to look at was a kind of socialism, but a democratic form of socialism."

There was a certain logic to such a development in the vision of a man who had committed himself unequivocally to the empowerment of the poor, to the transformation of the nation, away from racism, from militarism and materialism, toward a more humane and compassionate way of life. But this was a heavy burden to place on a staff and on supporters who had not originally signed up for such a perilous, uncharted, transformative journey. What did it mean to "compel unwilling authorities to yield to the mandates of justice," especially when the authorities were no longer in Birmingham, Alabama, Greenwood, Mississippi, or St. Augustine, Florida, but at the highest levels of the nation's political, economic, and military structures? Beyond this voice ("increasingly at odds with the rest of American society") and this vision, shaped in the fierce cauldron of American poverty, what was the way, in such a time, "to redeem the soul of America"?

King was unclear about how this would be done, but all through the post-Selma period he was in search. (Perhaps it would have been good to stop, to be quiet, to listen to voices from within. He often spoke of longing for an extended time of silence and retreat, moving toward the center of his being.) In the midst of the search, only one element of the revolutionary way ahead seemed constantly clear to him. Nonviolence had to be at its center—at least as long as he was involved in the struggle. Thus King was in search of a way that much of the world still deems impossible, the way of revolutionary nonviolence.

In the midst of the powerful explosions in Newark and Detroit and scores of other cities in the summer of 1967, in the midst of all the terrors of Vietnam and their toll on the nation's psyche, King's way seemed surely "at odds with the rest of American society." But Martin did not believe this way to be at odds with our deepest human spirit and greatest needs as children of God. Moreover, he said "The limitations of riots, moral questions aside, is that they cannot win. . . . Hence riots are not revolutionary." So it was up to SCLC, up to him, up to whatever believers in the power of nonviolence there may be, (up to us?). "We in SCLC must work out programs to bring the social change movements through from their early and now inadequate protest phase to a stage of massive, active, nonviolent resistance to the evils of the modern [American] system . . ." he said. Reflecting on, shaped by the Northern urban struggles that he had experienced since Selma, King said, "Nonviolence must be adapted to urban conditions and urban moods." He was saying that "nonviolent protest must now mature to a new level . . . mass civil disobedience. . . . There must be more than a statement to the larger society, there must be a force that interrupts its functioning at some key point. . . ."

This was King's way as he moved into the last fall and winter of his life. By then, he had announced that this way of massive nonviolent civil disobedience would become the center of his movement for the next major campaign—a return to Washington, D.C. He was improvising, groping, pushing his organization to move with him. His plan was to mobilize and train thousands of the poor and their allies to come to the nation's capital and "just camp here and stay" until the country's elected leaders acted on the urgent needs of the poor. In the great black tradition, he was improvising, but he kept moving, warning that "the city will not function," until Congress created and approved "a massive program on the part of the federal government that will make jobs or income a reality for every American citizen." In the fall, King was envisioning more than Washington as target. "We've got to find a method that will disrupt our cities if necessary, create the crisis that will force the nation to look at the situation, dramatize it, and yet at the same time not destroy life or property," he said. He was challenging the nation to face the poor, to turn from its insane war and face the poor, to turn from its materialism and face the poor. He was planning to bring the poor of every color, to stand and sit with the poor where they could not be missed. He said,

> We've got to camp in—put our tents in front of the White House. . . . We've got to make it known that until our problem is solved, America may have many, many days, but they will be full of trouble. There will be no rest, there will be no tranquility in this country until the nation comes to terms with our problem.

Yes, he said, again and again, "our problem." This was the voice and the way of the man who had chosen "to identify with the underprivileged . . . to identify with the poor . . . to give my life for those who have been left out of the sunlight of opportunity." He was coming back to Washington with them, but this time, he said, it would not be "to have a beautiful day." This time he was determined to create a new day, to begin a new time.

By the last months it was clear to Martin King that the vision of a new time, filled with a harsh and dreadful beauty of its own, would have to rise from a broad, ever-expanding base. For just as he had discovered that there was no way to address the needs of the black poor in America without attacking the structures of poverty-making which entrapped all the nation's poor people, so, too, was it impossible to isolate the American situation from its larger, international context. As a result, King continued to move beyond dreams, to declare,

> The storm is rising against the privileged minority of the earth, from which there is no shelter in isolation or armament. The storm will not abate until a just distribution of the fruits of the earth enables men [and women] everywhere to live in dignity and human decency.

Then, forever nurturing hope, forever seeing the best possibilities of the people who shared that cradle, that cauldron which had shaped him, he concluded, "The American Negro may be the vanguard of a prolonged struggle that may change the shape of the world, as billions of deprived shake and transform the earth in the quest for life, freedom and justice."

So he moved and sent his staff among the Native Americans, Hispanics, Appalachian whites, returned to the young black gang members of Chicago and Cleveland, attempting to recruit a courageous band of rainbow warriors for the still inadequately defined, but deeply felt, nonviolent army of hope. So he began to consider making connections with Latin American sisters and brothers who believed in the possibilities of nonviolent revolution, for he knew that our hope and our pain were organically connected to their own.

At the end, moving toward his rendezvous with destiny, King finally resisted all the powerful temptations to despair that tore at him from within and without. Speaking to himself and to others he said, "I can't lose hope . . . because when you lose hope, you die." At the end, moving toward his rendezvous with hope, he faltered, wondered if he should give up on the desperate move toward Washington, wondered if he should submit to the fears and disagreements within his staff and the hostility and anger that were being shouted at him from all the mainstream American nation, black and white, from all who prized order more than justice, from all who feared an uprising of the poor. But he kept moving, saying, hoping, convincing himself that there was nothing else that his integrity would allow him to believe, whispering, proclaiming, "We can change this nation. We can bring it up to the point that it will live up to its creeds." Indeed, as he pursued the unrelenting vision of a powerful nonviolent challenge to the center of America's governmental power, he believed there were some nonpoor Americans who would join him. He told his staff, "After we get there, and stay a few days [we'll] call the peace movements in, and let them go on the other side of the Potomac and try to close down the Pentagon, if that can be done." At the end, this lover of the poor, this pastor to America and its people, this explorer in the harsh and dreadful storms of compassionate transformation, refused to betray his vision, refused to allow his allies to seek shelter from the tempest, refused to turn from his own way.

The way led to Memphis, where garbagemen were marching for justice and dignity, where a bullet shaped and aimed by many hands was keeping vigil. In the midst of officially provoked violence and disturbing evidence of deep disarray within the Memphis leadership, five days before his crossing-over, King considered a Gandhi-like public fast, as "a way of unifying the movement and transforming a minus into a plus."

For reasons that are not fully clear (perhaps he wanted to leave the nurturing of such cleansing, empowering disciplines for us, in our time), King did not enter into the fast. Nevertheless, moving on, on his last night he stood in the midst of the people, with a storm raging outside, and declared that he had seen the promised land, testified that all fear was gone, that he was ready for whatever might come, for wherever he needed to go. And he told them that they would get to the promised land. (Did they—we—remember that there is no path to the promised land for those who forget their calling: "Let my people go that they may serve me in the wilderness.")

At the end, on the balcony, getting ready for his own movement forward, outward, as the American bullet was about to enter its chamber, King asked for a song. Faithful to the tradition that had shaped him, cradled him, prepared him, knowing what was necessary for his way, our way, he asked the band leader, who was rehearsing for the evening's mass meeting, to be sure to play "Precious Lord Take My Hand."

> Lead me on, Let me stand.
> I am tired, I am weak, I am worn.
> Through the storm, through the night,
> lead me on to the light.
> Take my hand, Precious Lord,
> lead me home.

That Memphis gathering never took place. King had another mass meeting to attend. So, to the accompaniment of a black gospel song and the sound of a rifle's shout, the brother kept moving, toward his rendezvous with victory.

Surely Heschel had known, had intuited it when he invited us. This was King's way, continually moving, even in stillness, grasping, being grasped by the loving hand of a justice-seeking, creator God—forever on dangerous pilgrimage toward the uncharted promised land that is always being created in the midst of the wilderness, calling others to join, to create, to overcome.

And just as surely, part of our response to the invitation must be to catch up with King. Because there are many ways in which we have not gone forward in the last fifteen years, we have tended to move, to be moved backward. For there is no stasis in nature. So we need to press on, to see as clearly as King did the challenge that American racism continues to present in all our institutions, built as they have been on white assumptions, Western values, often projecting the narrowest possible vision of America. He challenges us to catch up and move on, for now we must also deal with a temptation to racism which seeps into the black communities of the nation, especially in our responses to the new (and old) Asian Americans and Hispanics. Now we are pressed to take up the complex but not impossible task of creating a truly multicultural and multiracial society where power, responsibilities, visions, and burdens are shared.

We catch up with King only as we face all the hard contradictions of the militarism he decried, the militarism that provides comfortable contracts and salaries for so many good, middle-class people of every race and creed, and which provides survival allotment checks for so many poor families. We catch up and go beyond only as we challenge the public schools for equal time with the deceptive military recruiters, as we find the black, Hispanic, and Native American coworkers who must break the terrible grasp of the military's mystique on the lives of young people who see no other alternatives for themselves this side of prison, dope-dealing, or death. We go ahead by forging new images of peacemaking, new institutions for the development of agents of reconciliation, new research on the possibilities of nonviolent civilian defense of borders and homelands (until there are no borders and every land is home). We go ahead by exploring new understandings of the intimate relationships between peace and justice, between inner peace and external peace, between love in dreams and love in practice. We go ahead by creating reservoirs of peace within us, around us, wherever we are, in whatever family and community, preparing for the coming time of great flooding, watering the small places now.

We catch up and go ahead by recognizing all the ways in which we participate in the scourge of materialism that King so thoroughly condemned. We go ahead when we see more clearly what this passion for consumption and accumulation does to our Mother Earth, to our brothers and sisters, to our children yet unborn.

We go ahead—especially those of us who began our life journeys in the heart of the peoples of color of this land—when we recognize that "success" must be open to new, less individualistic measurements. We catch up when we take seriously King's words: "We are not interested in being integrated into *this* value structure." We go ahead when we realize that if we aspire to nothing more than the dark-skinned mimicking of America's destructive materialism, then we will have wasted our substance in riotous living, we will have betrayed the forbears who suffered so much to bring us here, and we will have failed the children who long to be born into a better place, a more loving, less threatening, more healing space.

We go ahead when we recognize much that King could see only dimly in his own time and place—such as the need to develop a society in which women not only continue to hold up their half of the sky, but are free to participate fully in the creation of a nation that neither patronizes, fears, nor abuses its females or its feminine spirit. To move on is to see the absolute necessity of protecting the life and rights of those who choose a way of loving that is outside the heterosexual mainstream—while lovingly challenging them concerning the implications of their choice. It is to see, as well, the need to challenge all lovers, of every persuasion, to move beyond the egoism of our private passions and open ourselves to that urgent new compassion and commitment which drives us directly toward the poor. For we develop our best selves as citizens, as a nation, we catch up and follow, only when we take seriously again King's call for "a radical reconstruction" of America, relentlessly turning the nation toward the needs of our poorest, most vulnerable people.

Early in the 1970s, one of King's closest and best-known coworkers reflected on the direction his friend and leader had been taking in those last perilous years of his life. In a private conversation, he said, "In a way, it was probably best for many of us who worked with Martin that he was killed when he was, because he was moving into some radical directions that very few of us had been prepared for." The man paused, then he added,

"And I don't think that many of us on the staff would have been ready to take the risks of life, possessions, security, and status that such a move would have involved." Then another pause, and the final reflection: "I'm pretty sure I wouldn't have been willing." To keep moving is to become willing, among and beyond ourselves, which draws us into the company of the committed, helping us to become voluntary companions, fellow travelers with our brother Martin. To keep moving is to carry, continue, and re-create the best revolutionary traditions of America.

Of course, what we also know is that the personal weaknesses of Martin King and his courageous band of coworkers are just as surely a call to us, a call to become stronger, to learn from the pitfalls as well as the mountains. So we move forward only as we discover in our own time and in our own experience a nonviolence that wells up from the deep, increasingly centered, and disciplined places of our personal lives. Indeed, there can be no reflection on King's way which does not open up to us the need for a path that expresses our own searching, expanding confidence in the healing power of the universe, in the presence of a loving, leading Power, exposing us always to the harsh and the tender, to the dreadful and the compassionate, prying our lives open to the evidences of things unseen.

Going ahead, then, surely means stopping, in ways that Brother Martin felt he could not stop. It means moving in such a manner that our inwardness is nurtured, fed, developed. Martin learned "through many dangers, toils and snares," that the principalities and powers against which we are ranged in the struggle for justice will not surrender to self-indulgent, undisciplined, unfocused forces.

To go ahead means to search more faithfully than ever before for the inner resources on which nonviolent life and struggle must be based: the arts and skills of meditation and centering. The life-building practices of fasting and prayer. The nurturing of silence. The exploration of our own best personal and collective healing powers. The dancing, embracing, wrestling with our God, by whatever name—or silence—that being is known in our heart.

All these things, both in solitude and in company with fellow-seekers, now become more crucial than ever before. For ultimately, it is we and our children and our forbears, we and our great cloud of witnesses to amazing grace—it is we who must keep moving, to engage at every level in the continuing struggle which seeks to turn "the whole future of America" toward the last best movements of our brother, Martin, and then to burst beyond.

For those of us who are tempted (and who is not?) to doubt that such things are possible, for ourselves, for others, for our nation, we are helped as we try to remember, to break out of our larger amnesia. For all of our best religious and spiritual traditions in the human family carry the same supportive message: we are not alone in this struggle for the re-creation of our own lives and the life of our community. It has long been written and known that those who choose to struggle for the life of the earth and its beings are part of an ageless, pulsating membrane of light that is filled with the lives, hopes, and beatific visions of all who have fought on, held on, loved well, and gone on before us. For this task is too magnificent to be carried by us alone, in our house, in our meeting, in our organization, in our generation, in our lifetime. No, King knew, Gandhi knew, Malcolm knew, Dorothy Day knew, Heschel knew, Barbara Deming knew—and said, with mystics and physicists—"we are all part of one another," and we are all part of the intention of the great creator spirit to continue being light and life. That was what Martin saw on the night before his death. That was why all the fear had drained away. That was what Heschel knew in the midst of his call.

Now the grand and urgent challenge returns to us. Now we sense the deepest meanings of the rabbi's call, the brother's way. Perhaps now we are prepared as never before to hear the authentic voice, to catch the perpetually developing vision, to join the endlessly searching way. Perhaps now we are prepared both to catch up and move beyond, to run and not get permanently weary, to walk and not faint, submitting ourselves to the magnificent, continuing struggle to redeem the soul of America, beginning with our own beautiful, needy lives.

So we must keep going. For how else shall we mount up on wings like eagles? We must keep going, for how else shall we discover and explore the harsh and dreadful beauty of that radiant darkness where the wilderness and the promised land become one, where our way and the way of our brother converge? We must keep going. The whole future of America depends on it.

CHAPTER 7

BLESSED ASTRONAUT OF THE HUMAN RACE

On January 28, 1986, I had just arrived in Syracuse, New York, the closest airport to a school where I was scheduled to speak that night. An old high-school friend had asked me to take part in a King observance program at Cortland State University. On the way to the university we stopped for lunch at a restaurant, and as we were talking together about old times I noticed that there was something about the situation over at the bar—a kind of quiet and breathlessness—that caught my attention. I looked up at the television screen and saw the image of Tom Brokaw, looking very solemn. When I asked what was going on, I learned about the exploding tragedy of the Challenger Space Shuttle. I was stunned and not quite sure how to handle the images of fiery death.

Afterward I had a few free hours to rest in the motel and watch the television—half watching sometimes, half praying sometimes, allowing the constant replay of that disastrous scene to enter me, while trying to come to terms with what it might have to do with my lecture that night on the last years of Martin Luther King, Jr. Something beyond words and logic told me that there was a connection, though I didn't rationally know what it was. So I simply stretched out there and waited for whatever was to come. Before long the image of President Reagan appeared on the screen. Usually I have a great deal of difficulty in listening to

This was originally delivered as part of a series of lectures at Cortland State University, New York, in April 1986.

116

Reagan with charitable thoughts. But I'm very glad that I was trapped there in the room before that television, too passive to avoid hearing what he had to say. I don't know who wrote the words that the president spoke but there were two things that immediately began to grasp me and to make connections with my friend, Martin Luther King, Jr.

As Reagan was speaking, he seemed to be directing himself especially toward the young people of the nation. He said this about the astronauts whose lives had been taken so quickly: "*They had a hunger to explore the universe and discover its truths.*" Then he went on, and toward the end of his statement, in which he was speaking about the need to continue the program of space exploration, he said, "*The future does not belong to the fainthearted. It belongs to the brave.*"

Immediately the connection was made for me. Surely, whether he knew it or not, whether he liked it or not, Reagan was talking about Martin Luther King, Jr. For King was surely an astronaut of the human spirit. He, too, had a hunger—a hunger to explore the truths of the universe. He, too, had within himself a tremendous impulse not only to discover those truths but to hold fast to truth. *Satyagraha*—Gandhi's word for nonviolence—means holding fast to truth whatever the cost may be. And King, like the astronauts, sought not only to discover these truths and to hold fast to them but to attempt in his life to live and give full manifestation to the truths he said he believed. Like other astronauts of the human experience, he knew that truth unlived is not truth, that truth proclaimed in words alone cannot sustain us in our hunger.

My chance encounter with President Reagan reminded me that some of us tend to forget that there are ways of being explorers and pioneers other than the ways of technology. Some of the greatest discoveries in history have come from women and men who have been explorers of the human capacity for union with the magnificent creativity of God. That, too, is a marvelous exploration. That, too, is extraordinary pioneering. That, too, is great experimentation, to see what, if any, are the limits of the human capacity to be open to the grace and power and gifts of God. Our common experience is that we are satisfied with too little, with limits that are too low, with capacities that are too narrow, and the great explorers among us are constantly pushing us out beyond our narrow walls and saying to us, "You can be much more than you dream."

King was one of those explorers. And as I thought of the president and his statement about searching out the truths of the universe, I began trying to understand some of the fundamental truths that Martin felt particularly drawn to and bound by and compelled to try to live out. One of the most familiar was a truth that he put forward in the sermon that he preached on the last Sunday of his life. On that day he was at the National Cathedral in Washington, D.C. He was there partly because he had to explain to those very good and rather conventional Christian folks why it was that in a few weeks he was going to be coming back to Washington with what they might consider a rag-tag band of the poor.

Near the beginning of his sermon King spoke about a truth that he really believed. He said that through our scientific and technical genius we have made of this world a neighborhood, and yet we have not had the ethical commitment to make of it a brotherhood, a sisterhood. Somehow, in some way, he said, we have got to do this. Paraphrasing an earlier American explorer, King declared that we must all learn to live together as sisters and brothers, or we will all perish separately as fools. Here is the way that he so often put forward this truth that he believed: "We are tied together in a single garment of destiny, caught in an inescapable network of mutuality, and whatever affects one directly, affects all indirectly. For some strange reason I can never be what I ought to be until you are what you ought to be. You can never be what you ought to be until I am what I ought to be. This is the way God's universe is made. This is the way it is structured."

That for King was an inescapable truth, the fact that we are one through our relationship to the loving Mother/Father God. We are one whether we like it or not, but our oneness will not have its

In March 1968 King joins a march in support of striking sanita-
tion workers in Memphis, Tennessee.

fullest realization until we do like it and like it so much that we organize our lives toward the creative manifestation of that truth. This is what King was believing. This is a truth that he was holding on to.

The second important truth for King was his belief that he was called to be a minister of God through Jesus Christ. If taken seriously, of course, this is a daunting and dangerous belief. When King was at his best it was clear that he held fast to that truth, regardless of where it led him.

These were two of the major truths that King had begun to apprehend, and there was no one about whom it could be more fully said, that he had a hunger to explore the universe and discover its truths. We could add that once this man had begun to apprehend the truths of the universe then nothing could stop him from soaring on to explore the direction in which these truths might lead the human family.

King spent his life exploring the unknown possibilities, not primarily for himself, but for his beloved country and for his beloved humankind. It took much courage to be an astronaut. It took much grace and much faith to explore the unknown, especially in a country and a time like ours. But I think if we would appreciate Martin King adequately we must place him in that context of the great explorers.

As he moved across the face of the country what he constantly saw were the many ways in which racism, poverty, and militarism were consistently denying the truths of God. Therefore, he felt he had no choice. He had to hold fast to the truth in the face of the denials and the denyers. Even when the denials were official government policy and the denyers were the leaders of the nation, he had to hold fast to truth. Even when the denyers were brothers and sisters in his church community, he had to hold fast to the truth. Even when the denyers said that it is alright to kill God's children sometimes, especially if they're communists, he had to hold fast to the truth—to the reality that he believed to be the truth of the universe because, as he understood it, he was called to a ministry that was a ministry of prophetic, reconciling struggle. That struggle was the struggle to overcome these great scourges and denials of the human condition—racism, poverty, militarism and, in our own times, rabid anticommunism. It took courage, it took bravery to stand up as minister of God, as child of God, and to speak that truth and try to live that truth.

I would like to recall a couple of places where King obviously moved in the face of great danger to do this. In 1967, when most of the nation's keepers of conventional wisdom were still saying it was absolutely necessary to be at war in Vietnam, King stood up and spoke out and said that was a denial of the love of God to which he could not consent and before which he could not remain silent.

One year to the day before he was assassinated, he was speaking in New York's Riverside Church, trying to explain why he was dissenting against his government's actions in Vietnam when so many people were telling him to stick to colored affairs, telling him this was not his business, that he was not qualified to speak about American foreign policy. He answered that he had to speak because he had to live with the meaning of his commitment to the ministry of Jesus Christ. He said,

> To me, the relationship of this ministry to the making of peace is so obvious that I sometimes marvel at those who ask me why I am speaking against the war. Could it be that they do not know that the good news of Jesus was meant for all men and women—for communists and capitalists, for their children and ours, for black and white, for revolutionary and conservative? Have they forgotten that my ministry is in obedience to the one who loved his enemies so fully that he died for them? What then can I say to the Vietcong or to Castro or to Mao as a faithful minister of this one? Can I threaten them with death or must I not share with them my life?

Then he finally came to his second truth. He said,

I would have offered all that was most valid if I simply said that I must be true to my conviction that I share with all men and women, the calling to be a son of the Living God. Beyond the calling of race, beyond the calling of nation, beyond the calling of creed is this vocation of sonship and daughtership and because I believe that the Father is deeply concerned especially for his suffering and helpless and outcast children I come tonight to speak for them.

At that point he took on the responsibility of trying to express some of the thoughts and feelings of the Vietnamese people as they faced the American forces.

But I want to return to that sermon on that last Sunday of King's life. Clearly he was struggling. He was standing in this great cathedral in front of a congregation that included many wealthy persons, a good number of whom were supporters of the status quo. Seeking to speak the truth in love, King went on to try to explain to them why he was coming to Washington out of the truth of the universe that was in his heart.

He spoke to them about the terror of racism in America and then immediately went on. He said,

There is another thing closely related to racism that I would like to mention as another challenge. We are challenged to rid our nation and the world of poverty. Like a monstrous octopus, poverty spreads its nagging, prehensile tentacles into hamlets and villages all over our world. They are ill-housed. They are ill-nourished. They are shabbily clad. I have seen it in Latin America. I have seen it in Africa. I have seen this poverty in Asia. I have seen them here and there. I have seen them in the ghettos of the North. I have seen them in the rural areas of the South.

This man with eyes that refused not to see. "My God, I have seen them in Appalachia. I have seen them in the process of touring many areas of our country and I must confess that, in some situa-

tions, I have literally found myself crying." This man who refused
to close his eyes to the poor.

He tried to explain to the people of the Episcopal National
Cathedral why his truth would not allow him to back away, not
only from the poor, but from the causes of poverty. He was like
Bishop Helder Camara of Brazil, who has said a number of times,
"When I gave charity to the poor, people called me a saint. But
when I asked *why* men and women are poor, people called me a
communist." This was King exploring what the love of God and
the unity of the human family means in the midst of tremendous
inequality and injustice in this country.

So he came to his brothers and sisters in that great church, and
spoke to them from the explorer's truth in his heart, and he said,
"There is nothing new about poverty. What is new is that we now
have the techniques and the resources to get rid of poverty. The
real question is whether we have the will." He was speaking to his
fellow Christians—declaring that there was no question about
whether God willed that suffering should be done away with,
asking whether we have the will to enter into God's will and so
open ourselves to the truth, whatever the cost may be.

King was not quite sure where his exploration of this Divine
truth might lead, what it would do, where the astronaut in him
would go. He simply announced, like some well-dressed John the
Baptist, that in a few weeks some folks would be coming to
Washington to see if the will was still alive in this nation, in that
church. We are coming to Washington in a poor people's campaign, he said.

> Yes, we are going to bring the tired, the poor, the huddled
> masses. We are going to bring those who have known long
> years of hurt and neglect. We are going to bring those who
> have come to feel that life is a long and desolate corridor with
> no exit signs. We are going to bring children and adults and
> old people, people who have never seen a doctor or a dentist
> in their lives. We are not coming to engage in any histrionic
> gesture. We are not coming to tear up Washington. We are

coming to demand that the government turn itself to the problem of poverty.

The plan was for a continually widening, massive movement of nonviolent civil disobedience that would stop the operations of the American government until it turned itself from the killing in Vietnam to bring life to the United States of America. That was what King had in mind on that last Sunday of his life. "We are coming to engage in dramatic nonviolent action to call attention to the gulf between promise and fulfillment, to make the invisible visible." Then speaking to his sisters and brothers there he said, "And I submit that nothing will be done until people of good will put their bodies and souls in motion."

King understood the dynamics of what can happen to a people who refuse to live out the truth that they say they believe. So he was experimenting. He was exploring. He was stumbling, but he was continuing bravely to move out beyond the conventional limits of social action. In fact, what he was doing by that spring of 1968 was trying to go beyond even his own best wisdom, his own best successes, taking risks, moving into the darkness. That's why, in what turned out to be his last words in the Lorraine Motel, he was asking the bandleader that evening to play "Precious Lord, take my hand. Lead me on. Let me stand." If you're not taking any risks, if you're not moving into any darkness, if you're not going into any uncharted waters, you don't need anybody to take your hand. You just follow the map. But King had put aside the maps of the past and was trying to create new maps through the grace of God and the courage of the brave. Therefore he needed his hand to be taken, and he needed strength to stand, and in the process he was expanding his own being and calling other people to become much more than they dreamed they could be. He was calling us all to fly. He was calling us to soar. He was calling us perhaps to fall but in the process to become pioneers in the realm of human community, in the realm of human compassion, in the realm of human justice. He was doing all of this—understand this—he was doing all of this as a part of holding on to the truth of God's unifying, all-encompassing love. He was doing all of this while holding on to the insane, impractical, magnificent truth of the call to ministry.

Martin King was not playing games by the end of his life. He saw that we have systemic problems in this society and that they must be addressed. He knew they would not be addressed with bandaids. He was convinced that there has to be a deep shaking of the foundations of the nation itself, perhaps a second American revolution in which economic rights and responsibilities will become at least as important as political rights and responsibilities.

King, the astronaut, was exploring the way. Here is what he said to his staff in the summer of 1967 as they gathered together for the last SCLC convention of his life. He spoke of the need for the movement to address the question of restructuring the whole of American society:

> There are forty million poor people here, and one day we must ask the question, why are there forty million poor people in America? When you begin to ask that question you are raising questions about the economic system, about a broader distribution of wealth. When you ask that question you begin to question the capitalistic economy. I am simply saying that more and more we've got to begin to ask questions about the whole society. We are called upon to help the discouraged beggars in life's market place, but one day we must come to see that an edifice which produces beggars needs restructuring. It means that questions must be raised. You see, my friends, when you deal with this you begin to ask the question, who owns the oil? You begin to ask the question, who owns the iron ore? You begin to ask the question, . why is it that people have to pay water bills in a world that is two-thirds water? These are the questions that must be asked.

Here was the astronaut moving out into dangerous territory, territory where he would be labeled, as was Jesus, a subverter of the people.

King, the astronaut, was trying to explore so many questions: How do you come to a real sharing of political power in a society like this? How do you develop a new America where there is real, mutually respectful, cultural pluralism? How can you talk seriously about both revolution and nonviolence? That was the greatest challenge that King was struggling with in his last astronaut days, for he had come to believe that revolution in America, for America, was absolutely necessary, but he also believed that the only true revolution is a revolution that manifests the spirit of Jesus of Nazareth—nonviolent, loving, determined, defiant, and compassionate. How does one put those together?

At the end, King was still bravely exploring these questions. He was firmly holding on to what he believed to be the truth of the universe, and he was moving out in that truth and calling others to move out with him. That was one of the powerful things about him, this great mobilizing power that he had. He was always calling, calling us to move together toward a land that we have not yet known, calling us to re-create a just, compassionate, peacemaking America, to explore the borders and the heartland of a new nation.

On the night of his assassination, with a sense of what might be very close to him, he could still call others, call them to the great uncharted path. In the big church in Memphis, speaking to thousands of black people who had gathered together on a very rainy, stormy night, King spoke these words of encouragement.

Let us rise up tonight with a greater readiness than ever before. Let us stand with a greater determination than ever before and let us move on in these powerful days, these days of challenge, to make America what it ought to be. We have an opportunity to make America a better nation and I want to thank you and I want to thank God for allowing me to be here with you.

And then the end.

We've got some difficult days ahead but it doesn't matter with me now. Because I've been to the mountain top. And I don't mind. Like anybody, I would like to live a long life. Longevity has its place. But I'm not concerned about that now. I just want to do God's will. And he's allowed me to go up to the mountain and I've looked over and I've seen the promised land. I may not get there with you but I want you to know tonight that we as a people will get to the promised land. And I'm happy tonight. I'm not worried about anything. I'm not fearing any man. Mine eyes have seen the glory of the coming of the Lord.

Less than twenty-four hours later the astronaut moved on, following the vision his eyes had seen, claiming the future for all the brave explorers of hope.

Chapter 8

TELL THE CHILDREN

Ever since our forebears took on the awesome responsibility of nurturing children into maturity, we parents have been storytellers. And whenever we narrate the stories of spiritually powerful men and women who have lived among us, we step up to a beautiful calling, a humanizing gift, a truly parental vocation. For in exploring the lives of heroes and heroines we are able to introduce our young to the specialness of their own lives and to the great possibilities for triumph and tragedy that are stored within them.

Every third Monday in January, history compels us to observe the birth and the life of an extraordinary figure, Dr. Martin Luther King, Jr. By telling his story, we not only pay tribute to the man and the momentous social movement he led; we teach our children critical lessons about courage, compassion, and the merit of sacrifice for the community, as well as the darker sides of hatred and betrayal in human affairs. And because King was an American leader, it is important to ponder him, to realize that in some fascinating, ironic, and empowering way that goes beyond congressional laws and presidential signatures, he may be the true national hero of our time.

I first met Martin Luther King, Jr., in 1958 at his home in Montgomery, Alabama. My wife, Rosemarie, and I later lived around the corner from Martin and his family in Atlanta, and we marched with them during the 1960s. After Martin was assassinated in 1968, his wife, Coretta Scott King, asked me to serve as director at the King Memorial Center in Atlanta. Over the years

Rosemarie and I have been asked by thousands of children, teachers, and parents to share the story of Martin Luther King, Jr. And over time our message, our suggestions for how parents can best render both the man and his message, have come to this:

Start by letting children know that Martin was once a bright, sensitive, high-spirited child growing up in segregated, Depression-racked Atlanta in the 1930s. Despite the harsh realities of the time, Martin's primary experience was shaped by being part of a family in which he, along with his older sister, Christine, and his younger brother, A.D., was generously loved, nurtured, taught, disciplined, and sometimes spoiled. Children should know that Jennie C. Williams, Martin's maternal grandmother, lived with the King family in the heart of Atlanta's African-American community and that she provided much of the special community and care that children need.

Young people can also be helped to imagine how important Ebenezer Baptist Church was to the boy Martin, especially since his daddy was the pastor there. Thanks to the church, the Kings enjoyed an extended family of hundreds of caring, admiring parishioners.

Today's children will want to know that Martin loved school. And he loved to play. Dancing was another passion of his—although he often had to enjoy this pastime on the sly, for a preacher's son was not supposed to dance in those days. He liked girls too much to miss out on the opportunities for smooth words and warm contact provided by the dances of the forties.

Children will also be intrigued to know that Martin, like most youngsters, did not always do as he was expected or told. In fact, one afternoon during high school, he decided to sneak away from his homework assignment to watch a parade. That same day, his beloved Grandma Williams, who was already ailing, suddenly took a turn for the worse. By the time he returned home, she was dead. After that, Martin considered her death a punishment for his decision to steal away from homework, and he lived with a sense of guilt for a while. But in the end, those who watched him grow remember mostly a well-balanced young man who did not let his status as a preacher's son stop him from having a good time.

At the same time, Martin learned some early, disturbing lessons about racial, economic, and personal injustices. He saw the Jim Crow public toilets, the segregated movie balconies. He heard the hostile shouts of bus drivers demanding that he sit in the back. And perhaps because he watched his own father confront these inequities and survive, he refused to ignore them himself. Two incidents, in particular, bear retelling. Once, Martin and his father walked into a downtown Atlanta shoe store and sat down in the front section, waiting to be helped. When a white clerk tried to shunt them to "the colored section" in the back of the store, Martin watched with a mixture of confusion, fear, and pride as the Reverend King, Sr., announced: "We'll either buy shoes sitting here, or we won't buy shoes at all." They soon walked out without shoes, but with a large supply of personal dignity.

In another incident, young Martin witnessed his father's reaction as a white traffic patrolman stopped their car on the street, addressing the Reverend with a customary, "All right, boy, pull over." Daddy King responded by pointing a finger toward his son: "This is a boy, I'm a man. And until you call me one, I will not listen to you." They left that face-off with a traffic citation and a powerful memory.

It was through encounters like these that Martin gained a clear sense of his father's courage and resistance to injustice. During those same childhood days, he also witnessed his father's leadership in campaigns to register voters, to get equal pay for black teachers, and to feed the hungry in hard times. This role of the loving father as an effective pastor and organizer was never lost on young Martin. So by the time he was in college, Martin Luther King, Jr., decided that he, too, would be a Christian minister committed to changing society. The ministry King chose was a calling not only to serve the Divine Creator, but to serve other human beings, especially those in need.

April 3, 1968, King with Hosea Williams, Jesse Jackson, and Ralph
Abernathy on the balcony of the Lorraine Motel in Memphis the
day before he was shot.

Nearly all of the good that King did in this world grew out of these twin commitments.

When we tell children of King's development in Montgomery, Alabama, where he was called upon to be the minister of a church, the message becomes ever more rich and profound, for this chapter in his life reveals the deeply symbiotic connections between leaders and their communities. It was the African-American community in Montgomery, for example, that first organized on behalf of Rosa Parks—the unassuming but committed activist and seamstress whose refusal to give up her seat for white passengers on a bus led to her arrest in 1955. Indeed, this community first responded to the moment by calling for a bus boycott; then the largely unsung community leaders turned to King and asked him to be their leading spokesman.

Let it be known that the local heroism of Montgomery's African Americans prompted King to respond to his own heroic calling. Courage inspired courage. His family, too, was courageous; Martin and Coretta understood early on that such leadership meant putting Martin's safety and that of their family in great jeopardy. But these two young pioneers—it should be emphasized that there is no way to tell our children about Dr. King without recognizing how central Coretta was to his life—decided, just as King, Sr., had decided before them, that some things were more precious than physical life. They counted integrity and freedom for their children among them. Martin, Coretta, and the African-American people of Montgomery strengthened and supported each other, stood firm for what they believed was right, and took great risks for us all.

Do not hesitate to tell the children just what King's daring cost him, his family, his colleagues, and his followers: His house was bombed; the church of his coworker, Reverend Ralph Abernathy, was bombed; laws were misused to put King and others in jail; and countless members of the movement, whose names we may never know, were beaten, maimed, arrested, even killed.

But King and the body of people he led refused to respond to violence with more violence. At every point they believed it better to meet destructive force with creative, sacrificial power, to challenge hatred with unflinching love and good will. Indeed, while still in Montgomery, Martin and Coretta took a tremendous leap of faith and realized the full extent of their beliefs at home: they decided to remove from their own house the pistol once bought for self-protection, acknowledging that their ultimate security could never be found in guns.

As parents attempt to reenact King's powerful and moving story, his experience with the children of Birmingham, Alabama, in 1963 makes for an inspiring example of service to the community. The Birmingham of the early 1960s can be honestly portrayed as a city in deep trouble, ruled by the concentrated, antidemocratic forces of white supremacy, segregation, injustice, and fear. For African Americans, living there meant having few public places to play, to sit and eat, or to try on a dress without risking insult, injury, and even life itself. King and his organization, the Southern Christian Leadership Conference, had been invited to lead a campaign that would release this city from the dragon of legalized, suffocating racism.

Talk to the children about King and his interracial group of freedom fighters and how they came to the city, armed not with bombs and guns to match—or succumb to—the forces of violence, but with organizing skill and immense faith and courage. Then, in May of 1963, after weeks of organizing and singing and marching and praying and going to jail, the tide was finally turned toward justice when the African-American children of Birmingham came out on the streets to join the struggle for democracy. Facing dogs and powerful water cannons, the children and their families marched in the streets, singing loudly, "I ain't scared of your jails [which they filled to capacity] 'cause I want my freedom." Later, in broadcasts and broadsheets around the world, we watched in horror as the Birmingham police force turned on its young. This became one of the prime events marking the beginning of the end of white supremacy's legalized reign in this country.

Include in your story an account of the sacrifice of four girls' lives, taken by a terrorist bombing of Birmingham's Sixteenth Street Baptist Church one Sunday in September of 1963. These four youngsters had just studied a church lesson entitled "The Love That Forgives." It was Youth Day at their church, and the girls—Addie Mae, Carole, Cynthia, and Denise—had left Sunday school early to help lead the main services. But Youth Day services never began. Instead a massive explosion ripped open the church and ended their lives.

Martin did not know these girls personally, but they were his children. They were killed in the course of a struggle that he did so much to develop and lead. So he preached at a funeral service for three of them with a very heavy heart and a renewed commitment to keep working for a world in which no one would think it right to kill in order to preserve a way of life.

Of course, our children should also know that King was occasionally uncertain in his leadership. For example, a dozen days before the dramatic fifty-mile march from Selma to Montgomery, in the spring of 1965, King wavered. At a gathering of hundreds of freedom fighters at their Selma church headquarters, King told the crowd that they would try to move nonviolently through a line of hostile state troopers. But other movement leaders report that King had already privately assured President Lyndon B. Johnson that he would postpone this move until a federal judge could declare the outlawed march legal. When King took his marchers to the Pettus Bridge in Selma, he faced the troopers, knelt to pray, and finally turned back to the church where they had started. This act surprised and deeply disappointed many, especially some of the younger activists, who perhaps never forgave King for what they considered a failure of leadership and a betrayal of trust.

But children need to know that leaders who are impelled by a profound sense of justice and moral conviction cannot be stopped for long by their own fears and uncertainties or even by their own serious mistakes. And so King and his followers continued to march and organize across the South. Make it clear that the movement he led was not one of black people against white people. Rather, the children should know that King's persistence, his willingness to live and die—but not to kill—for the cause of expanding democracy, and a similar spirit among his many coworkers, eventually drew thousands of white allies into the healing vortex of the movement.

Still, to the majority of Americans, it was one thing for King to carry on a human rights campaign mainly in the South and another to criticize his nation's actions overseas. When he began speaking out against this country's military role in Vietnam, he was called a traitor, attacked by friends and enemies, disparaged by President Johnson, and labeled a liar by J. Edgar Hoover, then head of the FBI. But he continued to speak out against the war, calling it a terrible attack on the needs and lives of the poor here and abroad.

On a final note, bearing witness to the legions of homeless, outcast, and ill citizens in our midst, never let the children forget that King's final, unfinished campaign was on behalf of the poor. He was trying to mobilize a nonviolent army of whites, African Americans, Latinos, Native Americans, and others to go to Washington and challenge our government to meet the needs of the country's poor. As he crisscrossed the country working on the Poor People's Campaign, he was often bone-tired and aching with fatigue. He was also very unsure about the practical details and concrete goals of the campaign. His staff constantly voiced their own doubts; indeed, the pressures to get King to cancel or indefinitely delay the planned spring drive were enormous.

In the midst of all this, King had to fight to keep his sanity and his sense of direction. He had to remember that beyond all the chaos, there were still a wife and four young children waiting, constantly waiting at home on Sunset Street in Atlanta. Sometimes the relentless pressure led him to bouts of depression, opened him to careless, desperate choices in his personal relationships, causing him to temporarily lose his focus on the family. But their love for him was deep, and they remembered how good it was to have him at home, and they waited. And while they waited, King kept going. So when the bullet of greed and fear and "law and order" finally arrived at its target, many of us who knew King were utterly heartbroken, and temporarily overwhelmed with anger, but not really surprised. We knew too much already about the vocation and trajectory of compassionate heroes.

But Martin Luther King's children did not yet know such things. When word of his assassination reached the house in Atlanta, tell the children that his oldest son, Marty, then ten years old, was devastated not just by the loss of his father, but by the notion that a man who tried to love so many could be brutally assassinated for no apparent reason. Tell the children what Marty knows now: that love and compassion are not shields against the instruments of physical destruction. Rather, they provide us with the power to stand and face the enemies of light; they generate energy to create perpetual starbursts of brilliant hope, even as we take our last breath.

So tell the children that King lives. Let them know that we saw him facing the tanks in Tiananmen Square, dancing on the crumbling wall of Berlin, singing in Prague, alive in the glistening eyes of Nelson Mandela. Tell them that he lives within us, right here, wherever his message is expanded and carried out in our daily lives, wherever his unfinished battles are taken up by our hands.

Let them experience the great, humanizing qualities of King's hope. Teach them to recognize the hero or the heroine in themselves. Teach them to nurture the compassionate, the forgiving in us all. And, in turn, whenever you see their acts of kindness, altruism, courage, and willingness to share, be sure to praise and reward them with words and deeds. Take care to let the stories of their goodness become part of the family lore. Let them know that these traits are valued at least as much as good grades, competence in sports, or other more traditional accomplishments.

Encourage the children: Study Gandhi. Study King. Study peacemaking. Study war no more.

Let the recent developments in the Persian Gulf remind our youth and us that the use of massive weaponry may bring immediate gratification, it may provide temporary solutions, but it also creates deep wounds that often take generations to heal. Let Martin Luther King, Jr., be our guide to the Twenty-First Century. Then, holding the children and keeping faith with our own best possibilities, let us move forward.

MARTIN LUTHER KING
AT THE MILLION MAN MARCH

In the course of all the understandable but essentially diversionary controversy that preceded the magnificent spiritual pilgrimage that was called the Million Man March, many people sought to put down the 1995 event by reminding us all of the historic March on Washington of 1963, and especially of the inspiring and electrifying presence of Martin Luther King, Jr. In those often well-meaning comments, especially before the men's march, it was assumed that King and his spirit would not be present this time. But just as many of us were wrong about most of our predictions concerning the 1995 march, we were also wrong in our statements concerning the absence of Martin Luther King. Indeed, one of the most powerful signs of an uncontrollable spirit at work in the march was the constant appearance of King all through that day.

On certain levels his presence was obvious and explicit. Many of the speakers made reference to him, and it is likely that Minister Louis Farrakhan surprised millions of participants and viewers when he brought King into the heart of his rambling but often moving presentation. At one point, not only did Farrakhan quote his supposed opposite number, he actually quoted God quoting King, surely the highest form of recognition. As the Muslim leader worked his way through a Christian-shaped theodicy, allowing the Divine Creator to explain the purpose for the tremendous suffering of Black people in America over the centuries, he had the Creator saying to the men on the Mall, "Yes, I allowed this [suffering] to happen. But Martin King, my servant, said, 'undeserved suffering is redemptive.'"

Then, claiming his own voice again, Farrakhan returned to one of King's hallmark visions, this time not calling the national hero by name, but clearly identifying himself with King's vision in a way that would have seemed impossible less than a decade before. Farrakhan said to the men on the Mall, "You are ready now to accept responsibility for more than the ghetto. You are called to lift up America and the world." Although the charismatic and controversial Muslim leader did not name King, anyone familiar with the hero's history surely recognized that theme of Black messianic vocation, a theme raised by many African American leaders in many times and places. But its modern mark was set by King, beginning with his first freedom sermon as newly chosen president of the Rosa Parks-inspired Montgomery Improvement Association in December, 1955. As a young Black man of twenty-six, King had the visionary courage to see American Black people injecting "a new meaning into the veins of history and of civilization." Now, at the Million Man March, Minister Farrakhan was at least temporarily breaking away from a Black nationalist tradition that had nurtured him—and that he had espoused—for decades, a tradition which announced that Black Americans were responsible only for the uplifting of our people and our communities. On the Mall in October 1995 he preached another message, a broader, more universal one. Was the spirit of Martin King upon him? Why not?

Whatever we think about such a question, one other element of King's spirit was unmistakable, moving far beyond any words. In a time when so many Americans, including Black men, had seemed to be impervious to the echoes of King's impassioned calls for a way of unselfish love to undergird all aspects of our lives, on the Mall in October that love became a central presence and testimony. From every age and class of men it was the same: "I've never felt such deep love in all my life." "I never heard so many Black men declaring their love for each other." "I never saw so many sincere expressions of love." In their eyes, in their smiles, in their hugs, in their mutual respect, in their shared hope, the Black pilgrims on the Mall were clearly serving as witnesses to the continuing power of what King had called our "strength to love."

Will the men now re-vision the hero, and themselves, and find him as another source of strength to change themselves and their world? At this moment that question cannot be answered, but there is no question that King was on the Mall. Where his spirit next emerges depends surely on our willingness to experiment with and explore his best hopes, especially his spirit of compassion for the outcasts and his creative determination to try to organize with them to develop a new creative force for healing themselves and the nation. Didn't King say, "You are called to lift up America and the world"? Or was that someone else? Or does it really matter?

As long as we know that the march was meant to strengthen us for our long, hard, magnificent struggle to transform this nation into the just and compassionate place that will nurture the best spirit of all our children, perhaps its alright to be uncertain about whether the call came from Farrakhan or King. Indeed, it may have come from both, and both men may have received it from the transcendent One who continues to call us all. If that is the case, then our own deep response becomes much more important than which man was the transmitter of the invitation to struggle and hope.

NOTES

1. The Inconvenient Hero

1. Carl Wendell Himes, Jr., "Now That He Is Safely Dead," in *Drum Major for a Dream* (Thompson, CT: InterCulture Associates, 1977), p. 23.
2. *New York Times*, January 15, 1979, 1:1, 15:1.
3. There are, of course, many sources for the historic speech. One of the most accessible is August Meier, et al. (eds.), *Black Protest Thought in the Twentieth Century* (Cincinnati: Bobbs-Merrill, 1980), pp. 346–351.
4. *New York Times*, November 3, 1983, 28:1.
5. Himes, *Ibid.*
6. Joshua Davis, Classroom Discussion, Swarthmore College, October 29, 1985.
7. Martin Luther King, Jr., *The Trumpet of Conscience* (New York: Random House, 1968), pp. 75–76.
8. The opinion poll information appears in Lewis M. Killian, *The Impossible Revolution?* (New York: Random House, 1968), p. 87ff.
9. Lerone Bennett, Jr., *Confrontation: Black and White* (Chicago: Johnson Publishing, 1965), pp. 244–245.
10. Arthur L. Smith, *The Rhetoric of Black Revolution* (Boston: Allyn and Bacon, 1969), p. 228.
11. There are a number of helpful accounts of Mississippi Summer. Two of the most sensitive contemporaneous witnesses were, Tracy Sugarman, *Stranger at the Gates: A Summer in Mississippi* (New York: Hill and Wang, 1966), and Elizabeth Sutherland (ed.), *Letters from Mississippi* (New York: McGraw-Hill, 1965).
12. One of the most powerful personal accounts by a participant in the Mississippi Freedom Democratic Party challenge is found in James Forman, *The Making of Black Revolutionaries* (New York: The Macmillan Company, 1972), pp. 371–411.
13. "Dr. King Bids West Act on South Africa," *New York Times*, December 8, 1964, 53:6.
14. Coretta King tells of the visit of Malcolm X in *My Life With Martin Luther King, Jr.* (New York: Harper and Row, 1969), p. 256; King's

comment about Malcolm is in David Halberstam, "The Second Coming of Martin Luther King," *Harper's Bazaar*, 135 (August, 1967), p. 51.

15. Halberstam, p. 49.

16. Martin Luther King, Jr., *Where Do We Go From Here?* (New York: Harper and Row, 1967), p. 112.

17. "Beyond the Los Angeles Riots," *Saturday Review* (November 13, 1965), p. 33.

18. *Ibid.*, p. 35.

19. A helpful account of King's work in Chicago appears in Stephen B. Oates, *Let The Trumpet Sound* (New York: Harper and Row, 1982), pp. 367–419.

20. See Oates, pp. 395–405, for one account of the Meredith March. King's own telling of the story, as well as his reflection on the meaning and significance of Black Power, appear in *Where Do We Go From Here?*, pp. 23–66.

21. Oates, p. 413.

22. There are many reprints of King's April 4, 1967, Riverside speech/sermon. Some of them, unfortunately, are in edited and abbreviated form—without indicting that. I am quoting throughout from one of the most accessible and accurate versions in "A Prophecy for the '80s," *Sojourners* 12 (January, 1983), pp. 10–16.

23. When King preached a version of the sermon at Ebenezer that spring, he evoked applause when he noted the difference in the response of "the press and the nation" to his calling for black nonviolence in the South and his plea for American nonviolence in Vietnam. With signs of anger in his voice, he said, "There is something strangely inconsistent about a nation and a press that will praise you when you say 'be nonviolent toward Bull Connor and Jim Clark in Alabama,' but will curse and damn you when you say 'be nonviolent toward little brown Vietnamese children.' There's something wrong with that press." Martin Luther King, Jr., "Why I Oppose the War in Vietnam," April 30, 1967.

24. An official, and often perceptive, view of the rebellions appears in National Advisory Commission on Civil Disorders, *Report* (New York: Bantam Books, 1968). Another, more politically informed interpretation may be found in Robert M. Fogelson, *Violence as Protest* (New York: Doubleday, 1971).

25. Halberstam, p. 46.

26. Oates, p., 445.

27. *Ibid.*, p. 446.

28. King, *Trumpet*, pp. 59–60. A close reading of this slim, posthumously published volume offers important insights concerning the direction in which King's life and thought were moving.

29. *Ibid.*, p. 14.

30. *Ibid.*, p. 15.

31. *Ibid.*, pp. 16–17.

32. Martin Luther King, Jr., "A Testament of Hope," *Playboy* (January, 1969), n.p., pp. 194, 231–34, 236. This, too, is a helpful document for its presentation of King's radical direction at the end of his life.

33. King, *Trumpet*, p. 17.

34. Quoted in Oates, p. 473.

2. Getting Ready for the Hero

1. *Drum Major for a Dream* (Writers Workshop, Inter-Culture Associates, Box 277, Thompson, CT 06277) is edited by Ira G. Zepp and Melvyn D. Palmer.

4. Beyond Amnesia

1. David J. Garrow, *Bearing the Cross: Martin Luther King, Jr., and the Southern Christian Leadership Conference* (New York, 1986), p. 524.

2. David Halberstam, "The Second Coming of Martin Luther King., Jr." *Harper's* 235 (August 1967), 46.

3. James M. Washington, ed., *A Testament of Hope: The Essential Writings of Martin Luther King, Jr.* (San Francisco, 1986). 189–94, 340–77; Garrow, *Bearing the Cross*, 539–40; Stephen B. Oates, *Let the Trumpet Sound* (New York, 1982), 367–69. For examples of such objections to King's critical stance. See Garrow, *Bearing the Cross*, 469–70, 496–97.

4. Oates, *Trumpet*, 473.

5. Washington, ed., *Testament*, 250–51, 285.

6. Martin Luther King, Jr., "Address at Holt Street Baptist Church," Dec. 5, 1955, Martin Luther King, Jr., Papers (Martin Luther King, Jr., Center for Nonviolent Social Change, Atlanta, Georgia).

7. For such language in King's speeches, articles, and sermons, see Washington, ed., *Testament*, 240–43, 250–51, 314–23. See also Oates, *Trumpet*, 441–42; and Garrow, *Bearing the Cross*, 553.

8. Garrow, *Bearing the Cross*, 581; Washington, ed., *Testament*, 314–15; Garrow, *Bearing the Cross*, 563–64.

9. For the full text of the central document, Martin Luther King, Jr., "Beyond Vietnam," Riverside Church, New York, April 4, 1967, see Washington, ed., *Testament*, 231–44. For an exploration of King's

movement toward his position of radical opposition, see also Garrow, *Bearing the Cross*, 527–74, *ibid.*, 550–64.

10. In a 1968 speech, King condemned "irrational obsessive anti-communism" in America. Martin Luther King, Jr., "Honoring Dr. Du Bois," *Freedomway* 8 (Spring 1968), 109. King, "Address at Holt Street Baptist Church;" Washington, ed., *Testament*, 241.

11. For instance, see Washington, ed., *Testament*, 240, 250, 315; and Garrow, *Bearing the Cross*, 552.

12. For a summary of the debate on poverty, see *Newsweek*, Oct. 21, 1985, pp. 84, 87. Examples of King's resolve to organize the poor for nonviolent militant challenges to the status quo are found throughout his post-1965 conversations, speeches, and writings. See, for example, Garrow, *Bearing the Cross*, 575–624; as well as Martin Luther King, Jr., *The Trumpet of Conscience* (New York, 1968), 59–64. For King's statement on the dispossessed, see *ibid.*, 59–60.

13. Garrow, *Bearing the Cross*, 581.

14. *Ibid.*, 580.

15. Cornel West, "The Religious Foundations of Martin Luther King, Jr.'s Thought," paper presented at the conference. "Martin Luther King, Jr.: The Leader and the Legacy," Washington, Oct. 16, 1986 (in Cornel West's possession).